吳大澂書系

吳大澂

督辦吉林邊務檔案文獻選編

吉林省檔案館◎編

吉林人民出版社

序

丹心懸日月，寸土盡寸心。

吳大澂（1835—1902年），字止敬，又字清卿，號恆軒，晚號愙齋，江蘇吳縣（今蘇州）人。同治七年（1868年）進士，授編修。歷任陝甘學政、河南河北道、吉林邊務幫辦督辦、廣東巡撫、湖南巡撫等職，後因在中日甲午戰争中兵敗遼南而被革職。吳大澂是近代民族英雄，也是清末著名的金石學家、古文字學家、書法家。他愛好金石，精於考證古文字，著有《恆軒所見所藏吉金録》《愙齋集古録》《字説》等，均有重要學術價值。光緒六年（1880年），吳大澂奉詔隨吉林將軍銘安辦理寧古塔、三姓、琿春等東陲邊務，據理力争會勘邊界，捍衛主權，推進了移民實邊、創設機廠等一系列守土固邊的革新措施，爲吉林邊疆地方安定、邊防穩固、領土完整、民生安樂做出了重大貢獻。

吉林省檔案館珍藏的反映吳大澂辦理吉林邊務相關活動的檔案共計百餘件，時間跨度從光緒六年（1880年）正月二十九日至光緒十六年（1890年）十一月。檔案涉及赴吉任職、籌建防軍、修築炮臺、創設機廠、改設驛站、採辦軍火、辦理荒務、會勘邊界、任免獎懲共九個方面內容，較爲全面地記錄了吴大澂在吉林幫辦、督辦邊務的革新足跡，反映了吴大澂克勤於邦、救亡圖存、赤膽忠心的家國情懷。

本書按照吴大澂在吉林幫辦、督辦邊務活動足跡，以專題形式將塵封的歷史圖文并茂地呈現給讀者。撣去浮塵，拭去灰燼，用檔案還原歷史的原貌，用檔案展現英雄的功績，既能讓吴大澂相關研究更具系統性、完整性、權威性，也能讓其忠誠擔當、革故鼎新、矢志不渝、精忠報國的愛國精神歷久彌新。

歷史的滄桑與榮耀已深藏於歲月深處，但光照千秋的先人聖賢、錚錚傲骨的民族英雄在吉林大地上留下了深深的轍印。吉林人民正以全新的精神面貌滿懷信心闊步向前，希望本書能够激發吉林人民的自豪感和自信心，成爲吉林乘勢而上、振興發展的不竭動力，賡續英雄之志，續寫時代華章。

吉林省檔案館

二〇二四年十二月十八日

凡例

（一）本書收録吉林省檔案館館藏吳大澂於光緒年間督辦吉林邊務檔案文獻一〇八件，包括奏摺、奏片，咨文等。

（二）因該書是在原始檔案基礎上轉録，為保持古籍整理的書卷气和歷史感，全書使用繁體字形式。

（三）嚴格按照檔案原件轉録，整體尊重原件，文字不作增減。轉録不妄改字，原件文字有訛誤以『（）』形式標出正確文字。

（四）同一字在檔案中有异体字等不同寫法，原則上遵照原始資料文字轉録。

（五）檔案中有繁、簡並存文字，亦照原檔案文字轉録。

（六）模糊、殘缺字跡用『□』標注。如果通過前後文能够補出殘缺字，則在補出的字外加『□』，如有漏字用『［］』。

（七）檔案原文中偶有疊字情況，爲清代筆帖式在謄寫過程中筆誤造成，均按照檔案原始形態轉録。

（八）檔案中有部分文字書寫屬書法字体，已按照規範字體進行轉録。

（九）本書輔文中的繁體字均參照『古籍印刷通用字規範字形表』。

本書編委會

目錄

吴大澂

督辦吉林邊務檔案文獻選編

赴吉任職

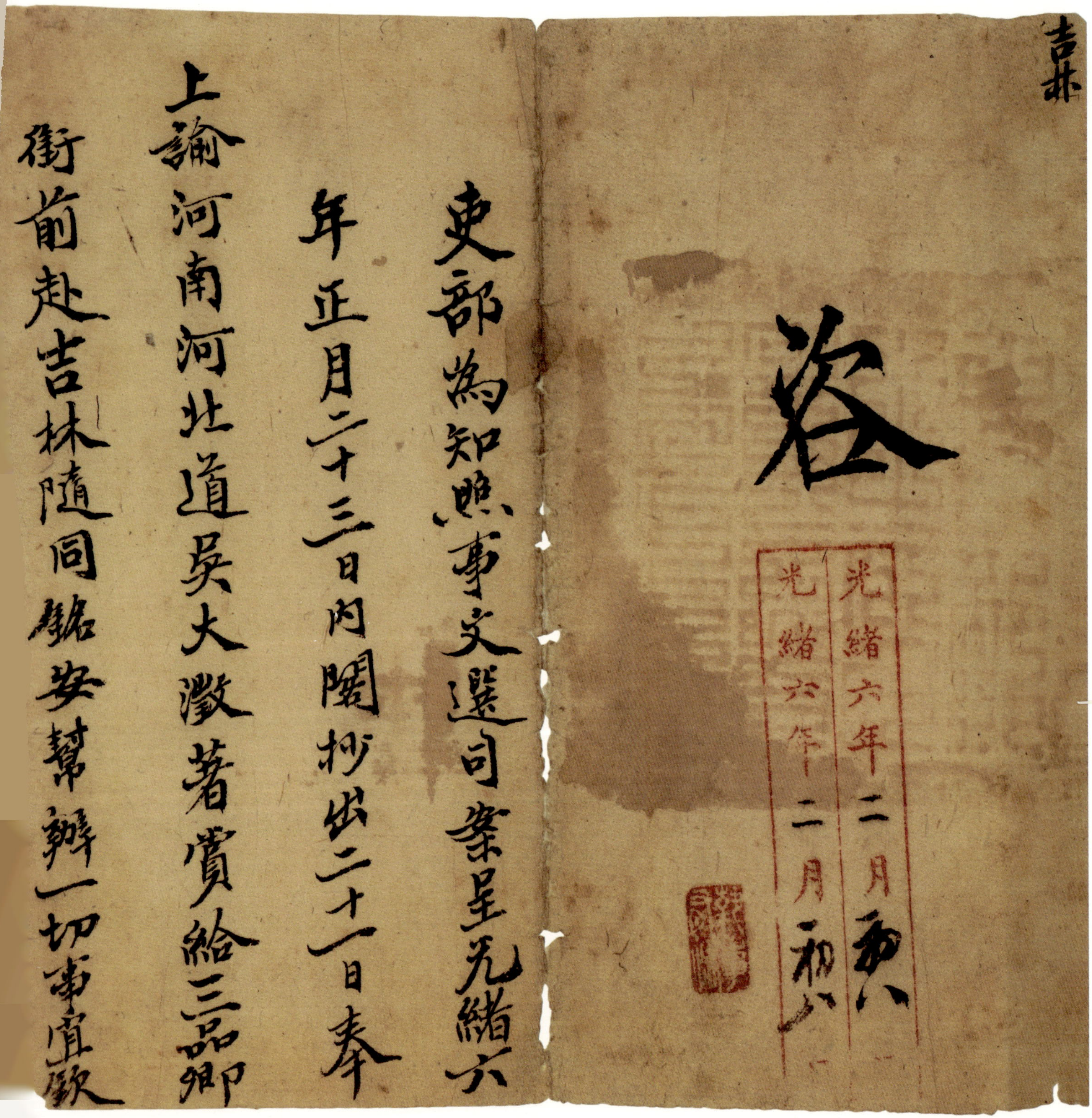
吉林

咨

光緒六年二月初八

光緒六年二月初八

吏部為知照事文選司案呈光緒六
年正月二十三日内閣抄出二十一日奉
上諭河南河北道吳大澂著賞給三品卿
銜前赴吉林隨同銘安幫辦一切事宜欽

光緒六年（1880年）正月，吏部為奉上諭吳大澂著賞給三品卿銜赴吉林隨同銘安幫辦一切事宜事給吉林將軍的咨

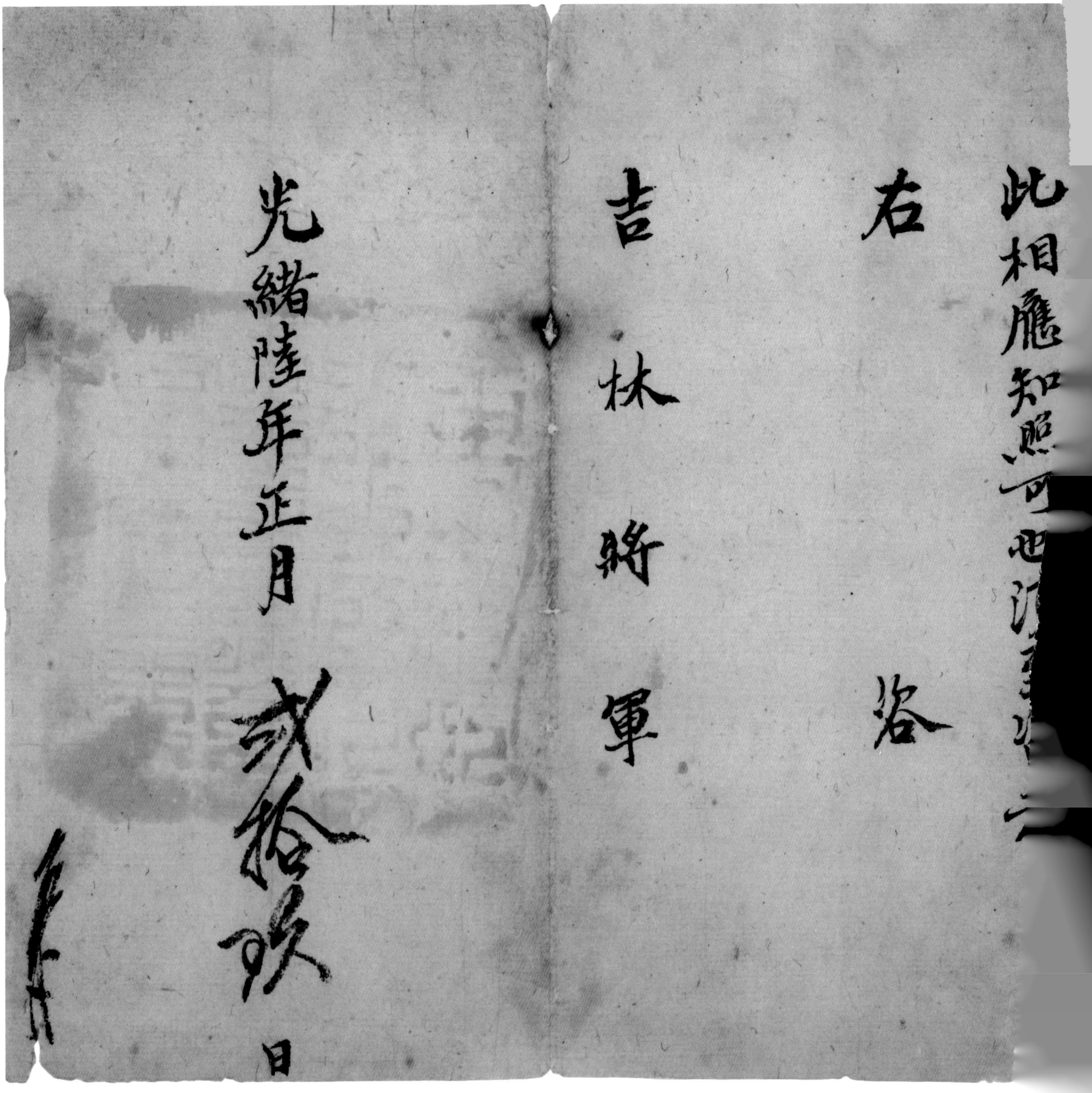

此相應知照可也須至

右　咨

吉林將軍

光緒陸年正月貳拾玖日

吏部為知照事。文選司案呈，光緒六年正月二十三日內閣抄出，二十一日奉上諭：河南河北道吳大澂著賞給三品卿銜，前赴吉林隨同銘安幫辦一切事宜。欽此。相應知照可也。須至咨者。

右咨吉林將軍。

光緒陸年正月貳拾玖日。

光緒六年（1880年）三月，河南巡撫涂宗瀛為河北道吳大澂奉旨來京召見起程日期事給吉林將軍的咨并抄片

兵部侍郎兼都察院右副都御史巡撫河南等處地方兼提督銜節制全省軍務並駐防滿洲營官兵兼理河道涂為咨明事。

照得本部院於光緒六年三月初八日附奏，前河北道吳奉旨來京召見起程日期一片，除俟奉到諭旨，另行恭録咨送外，相應咨明，為此合咨貴將軍，請煩查照施行。須至咨者。

計粘抄片一紙。

右咨吉林將軍。

光緒六年三月初八日。

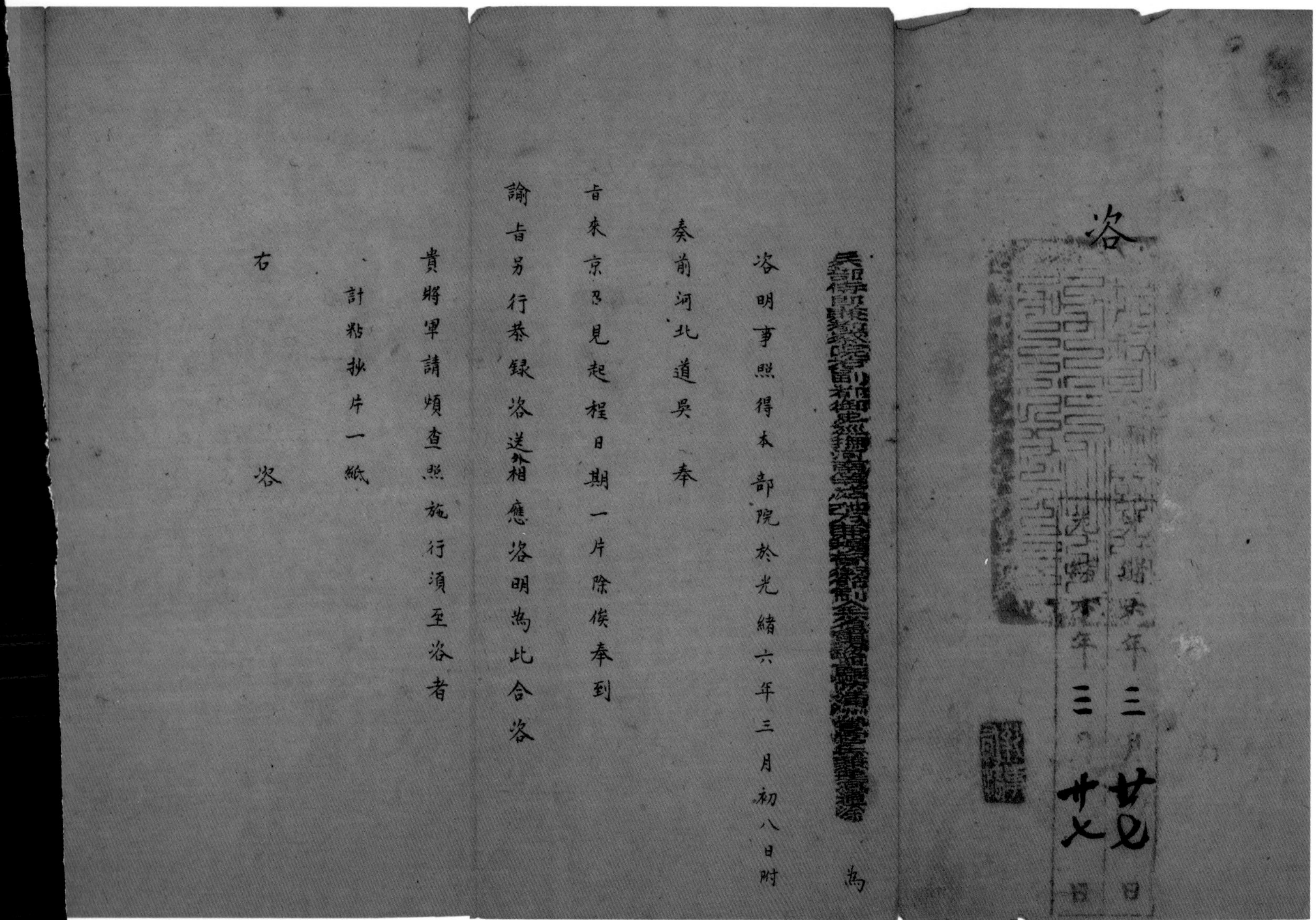

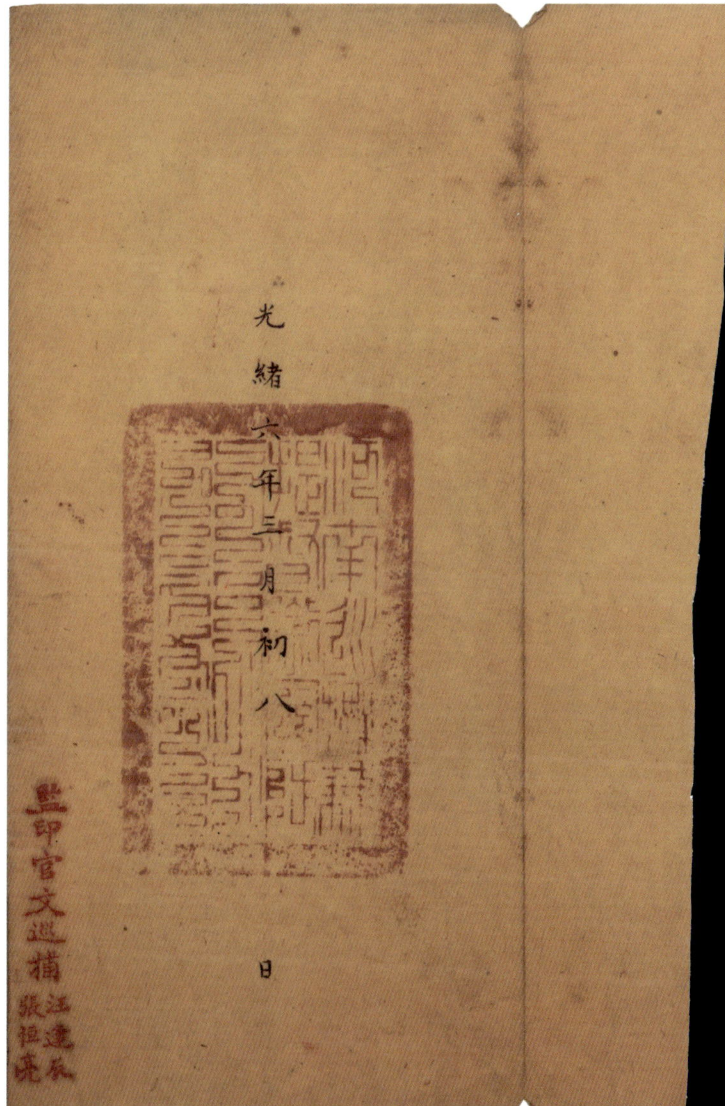

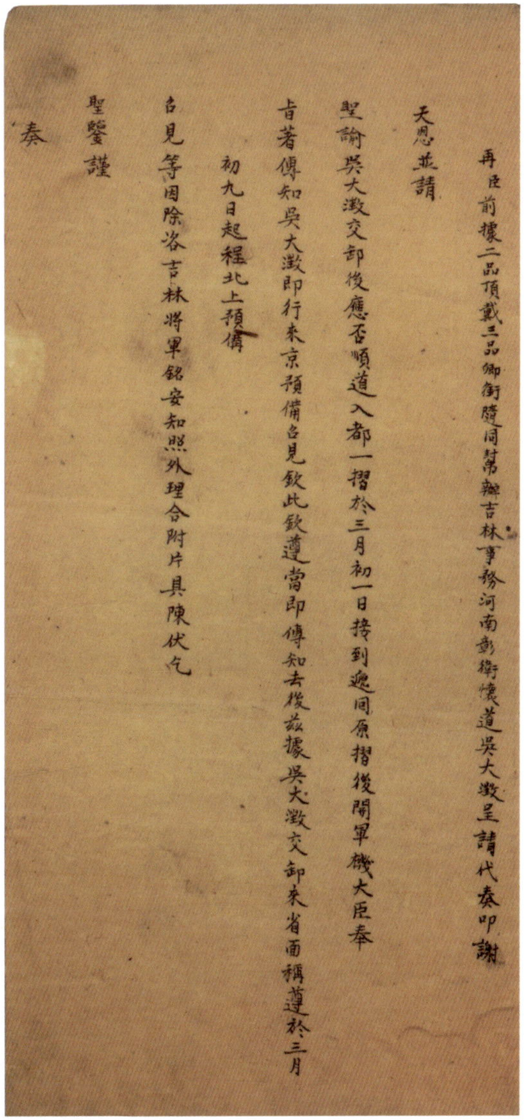

抄片

再，臣前據二品頂戴三品卿銜隨同幫辦吉林事務河南彰衛懷道吳大澂呈請，代奏叩謝天恩，並請聖諭，吳大澂交卸後應否順道入都一摺，於三月初一日接到遞回原摺後開，軍機大臣奉旨：著傳知吳大澂即行來京預備召見。欽此。欽遵。當即傳知去後，茲據吳大澂交卸來省面稱，遵於三月初九日起程北上預備召見。等因。除洛吉林将軍銘安知照外，理合附片具陳，伏乞聖鑒。謹奏。

光緒六年（1880年）三月，吉林將軍銘安為欽差吳大澂來吉幫辦一切事宜不日抵境飭照章預備妥為應付事給西路驛站監督的劄

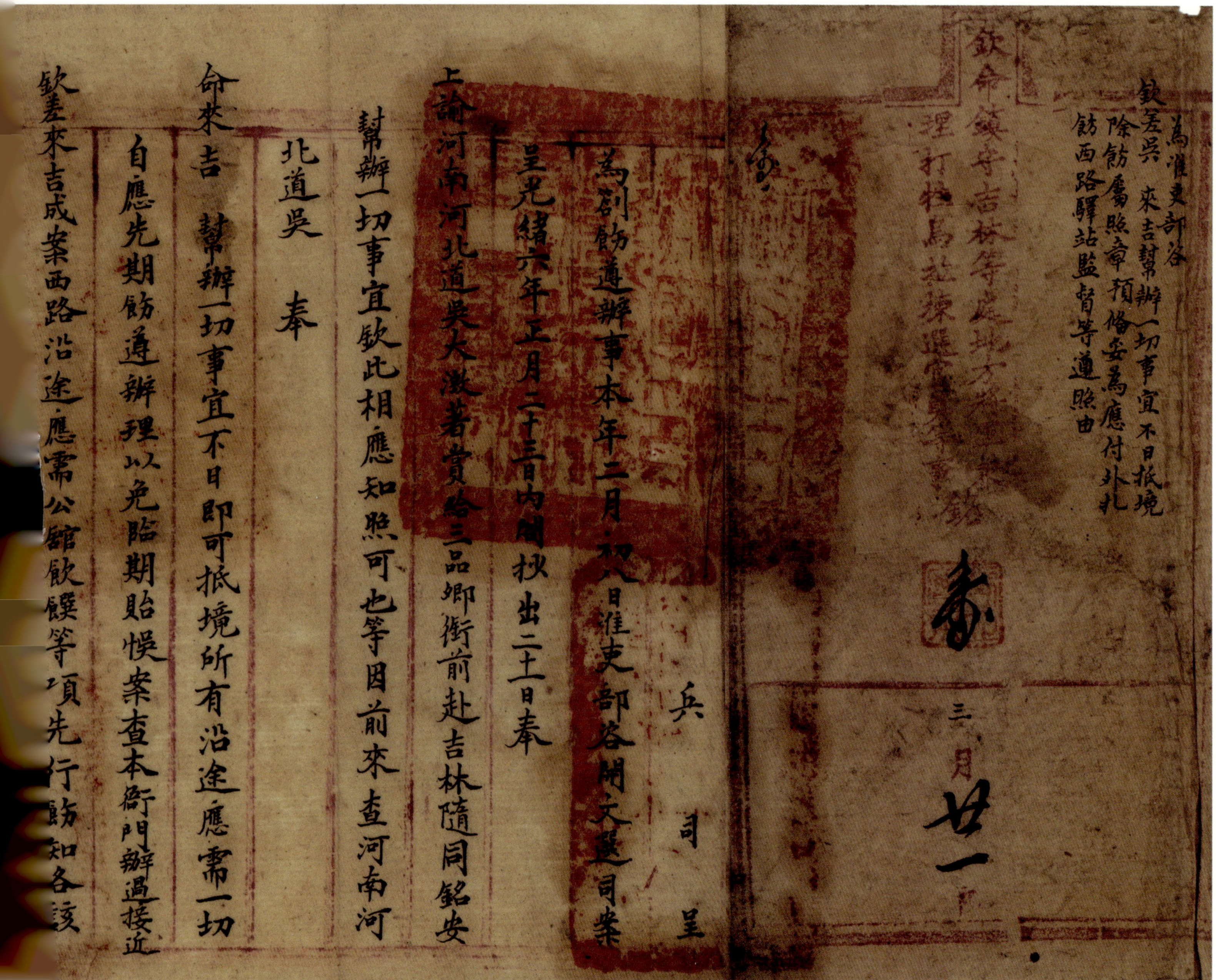

兵司呈，為劄飭遵辦事。本年二月初八日准吏部咨開，文選司案呈，光緒六年正月二十三日內閣抄出，二十一日奉上諭：河南河北道吳大澂著賞給三品卿銜，前赴吉林隨同銘安幫辦一切事宜。欽此。相應知照可也。等因前來。查河南河北道吳奉命來吉幫辦一切事宜，不日即可抵境，所有沿途應需一切自應先期飭遵辦理，以免臨期貽悞。案查本衙門辦過接近欽差來吉成案，西路沿途應需公館、飲饌等項，先行飭知各該地方官妥為預備守候，應付探接護送其經過道，如有難行處所，一体出派丁役按段修理，勿得稍有阻滯在案。茲准吏部行知，合行援案呈請，扎（劄）

飭吉林伯都訥同知、長春廳通判、三邊門章京等遵照面奉先期備辦，勿得臨期貽悞，并扎（劄）飭西路驛站監督轉飭西路各站一体照章預備齊楚(楚)妥為應付，仍將欽差抵境信息以及按日行程如何應付飛速報省，并扎（劄）飭二道河卡官，伊通佐領、巡檢等遵照一体按段近接護送隨時馳報外，相應由兵司移付户司查照可也。特扎（劄）。

由兵司移付户司。

劄吉林伯都訥同知、長春廳通判，赫爾蘇、佈爾圖庫、伊通等邊門章京，西路驛站監督、二道河卡官，伊通佐領、巡檢等准此。

光緒六年三月。

筆帖式全德註、雲騎尉榮祥對。

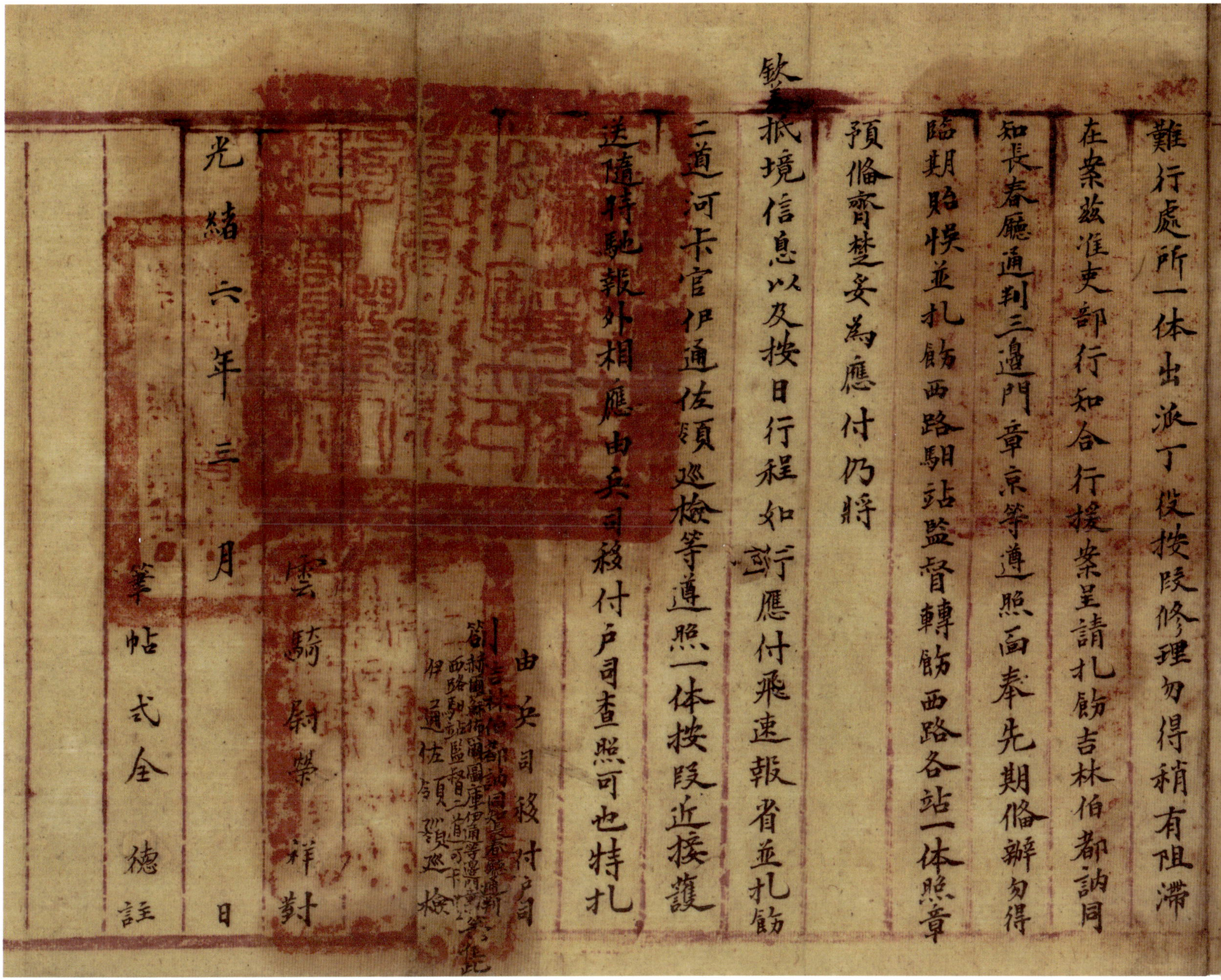

光緒六年（1880年）四月，欽差大臣直隸總督李鴻章為請調候補直隸州戴宗騫暫隨吳大澂赴吉委用事給吉林將軍的咨並抄片

欽差大臣督辦北洋海防事宜辦理通商事務太子太傅文華殿大學士直隸總督部堂一等肅毅伯李爲抄片咨行事。為照本大臣於光緒六月四月初七日在天津行館由驛附奏，請調候補直隸州戴宗騫暫隨吳大澂赴吉委用一片，除俟奉到諭旨恭錄咨行外，相應抄片咨會，為此合咨貴將軍，請煩查照施行。須至咨者。

計抄片。

右咨吉林將軍銘。

光緒六年四月初八日。

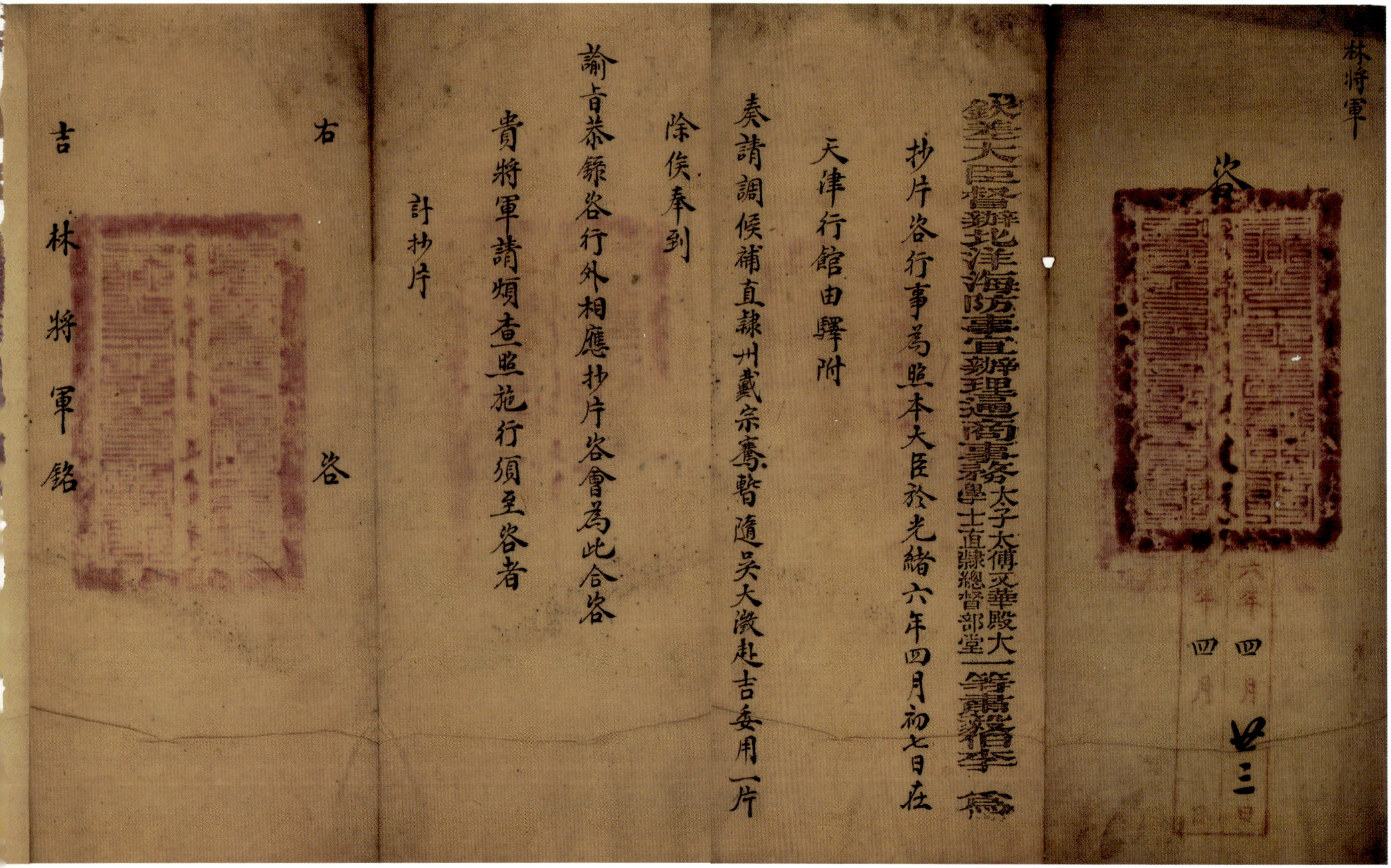
吉林將軍
咨
欽差大臣督辦北洋海防事宜辦理通商事務太子太傅文華殿大學士直隸總督部堂一等肅毅伯李 爲
抄片咨行事為照本大臣於光緒六年四月初七日在
天津行館由驛附
奏請調候補直隸州戴宗騫暫隨吳大澂赴吉委用一片
除俟奉到
諭旨恭錄咨行外相應抄片咨會為此合咨
貴將軍請煩查照施行須至咨者
計抄片
右 咨
吉林將軍銘

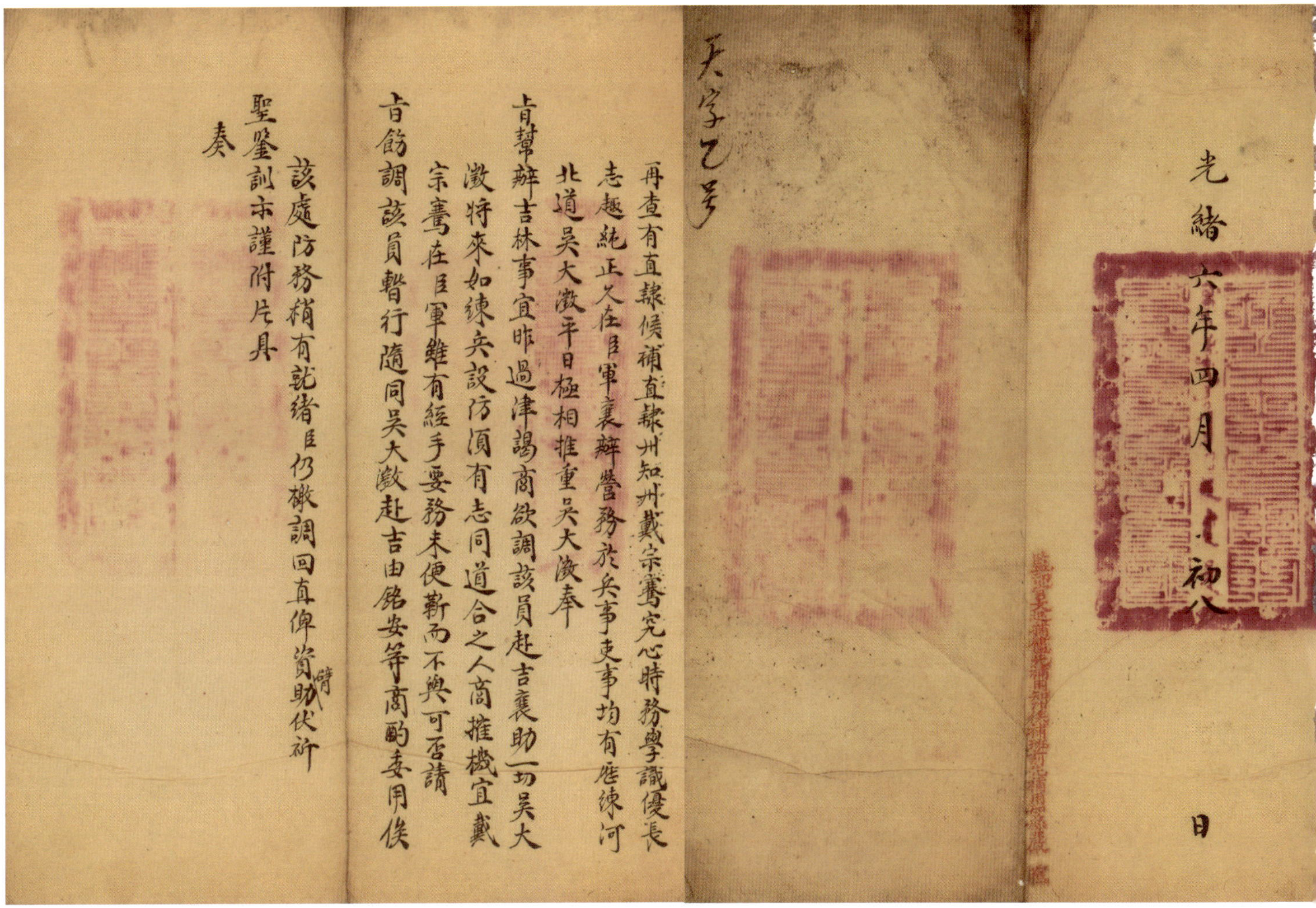
光緒六年四月初八日

天字乙号

再查有直隸候補直隸州知州戴宗騫究心時務學識優長
志趣純正久在臣軍襄辦營務於兵事吏事均有歷練河
北道吳大澂平日極相推重吳大澂奉
旨幫辦吉林事宜昨過津謁商欲調該員赴吉襄助一切吳大
澂將來如練兵設防須有志同道合之人商榷機宜戴
宗騫在臣軍雖有經手要務未便靳而不與可否請
旨飭調該員暫行隨同吳大澂赴吉由銘安等商酌委用俟
該處防務稍有就緒臣仍檄調回直俾資臂助伏祈
聖鑒訓示謹附片具
奏

抄片

再，查有直隸候補直隸州知州戴宗騫究心時務、學識優長、志趣純正，久在臣軍襄辦營務，於兵事、吏事均有歷（歷）練，河北道吳大澂平日極相推重。吳大澂奉旨幫辦吉林事宜，昨過津謁商，欲調該員赴吉襄助一切。吳大澂將來如練兵設防，須有志同道合之人商榷機宜，戴宗騫在臣軍雖有經手要務，未便靳而不與。可否請旨飭調該員暫行隨同吳大澂赴吉，由銘安等商酌委用。俟該處防務稍有就緒，臣仍檄調回直，俾資臂助，伏祈聖鑒訓示，謹附片具奏。

光緒七年（1881年）二月，吉林將軍銘安為幫辦吉林一切事宜及地方諸務事給吳大澂的咨

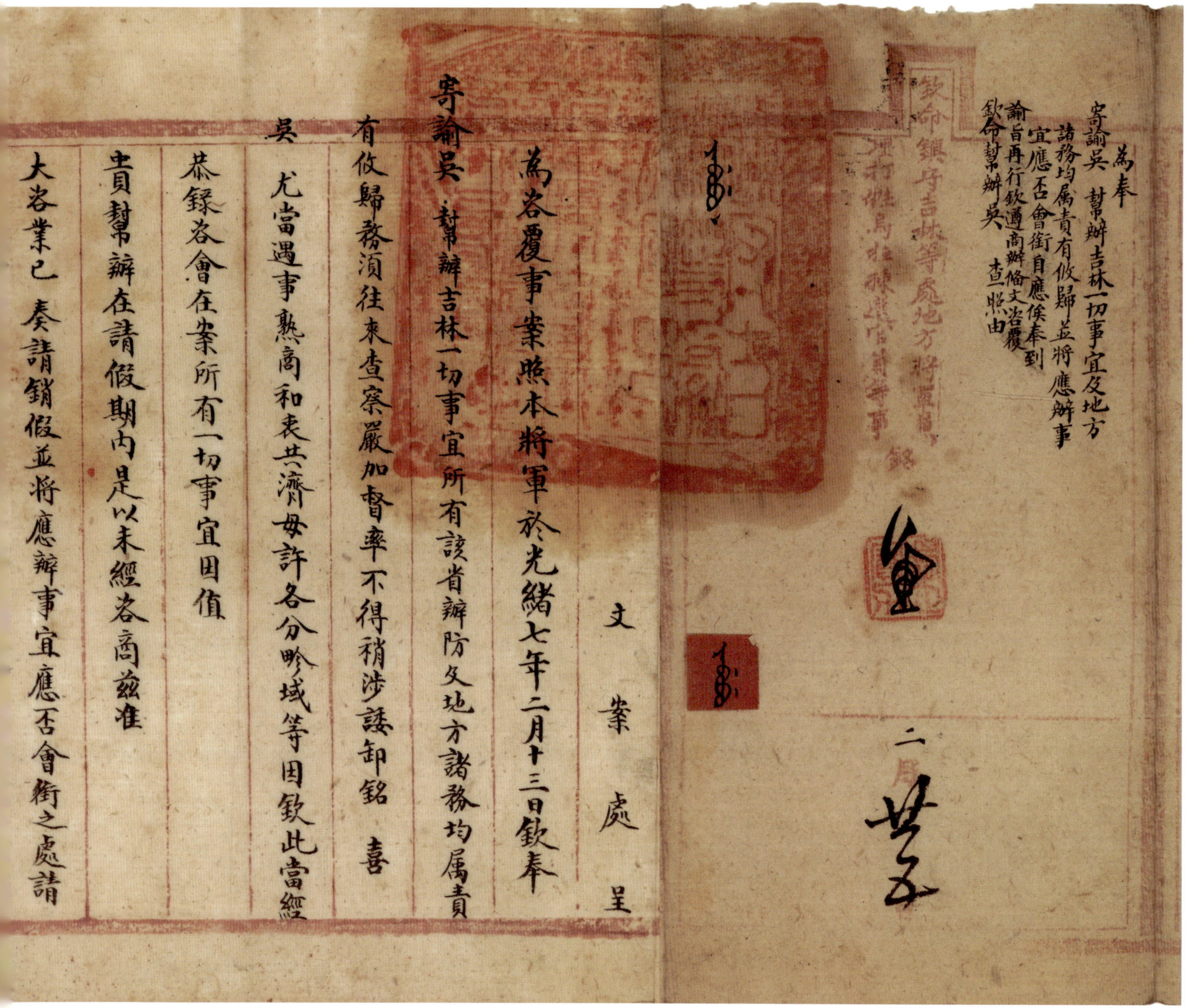

為奉
寄諭吳 幫辦吉林一切事宜及地方諸務均屬責有攸歸並將應辦事宜應否會銜自應俟奉到
諭旨再行欽遵商辦備文咨覆
欽命幫辦吳 查照由

文案處呈

為咨覆事案照本將軍於光緒七年二月十三日欽奉
寄諭吳 幫辦吉林一切事宜所有該省辦防及地方諸務均屬責
有攸歸務須往來查察嚴加督率不得稍涉諉卸銘 喜
吳 尤當遇事熟商和衷共濟毋許各分畛域等因欽此當經
恭錄咨會在案所有一切事宜因值
貴幫辦在請假期內是以未經咨商茲准
大咨業已 奏請銷假並將應辦事宜應否會銜之處請

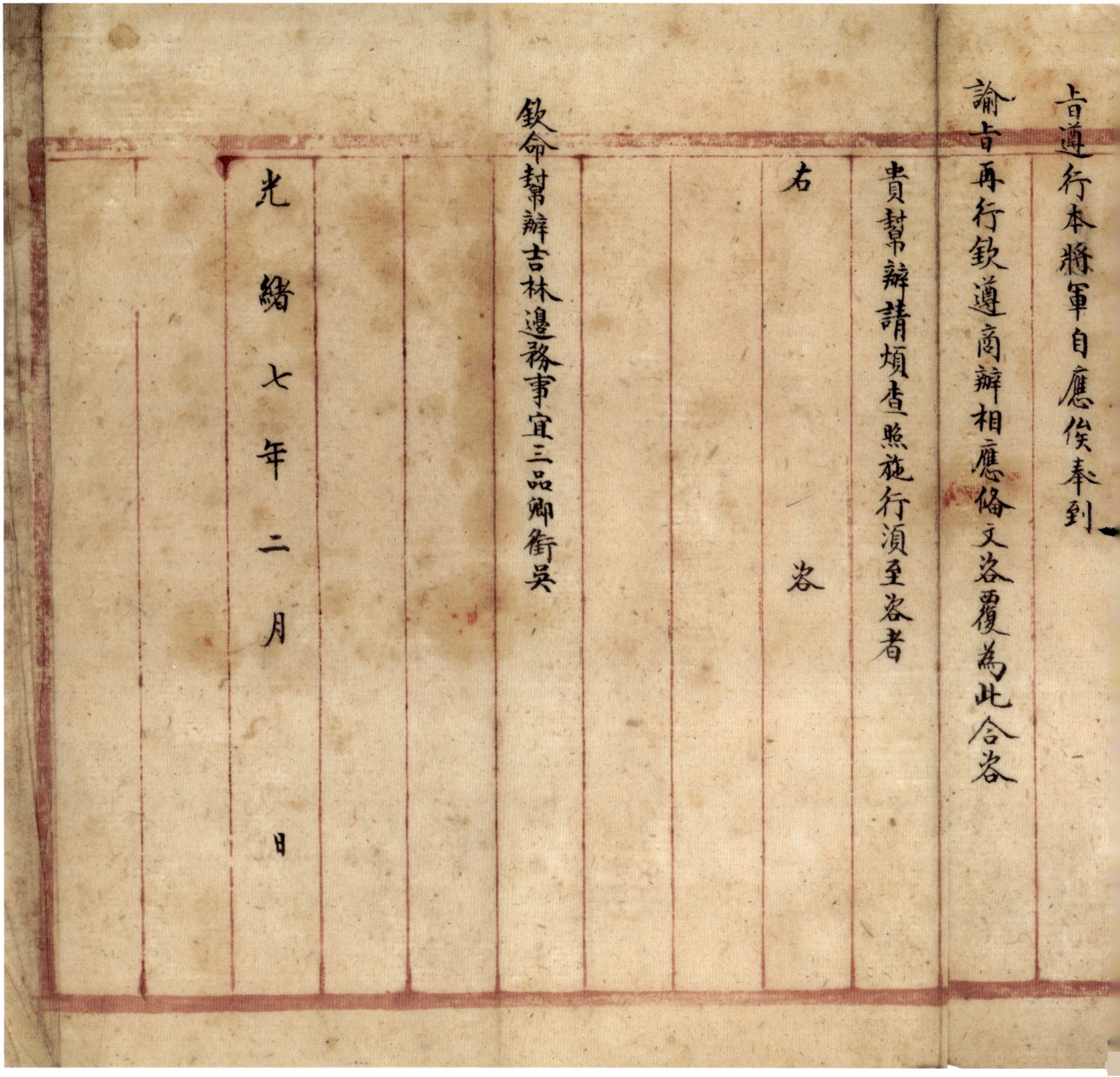
旨遵行本將軍自應俟奉到
諭旨再行欽遵商辦相應備文咨覆為此合咨
貴幫辦請煩查照施行須至咨者
右　咨
欽命幫辦吉林邊務事宜三品卿銜吳
光緒七年二月　日

文案處呈，為咨覆事。案照本將軍於光緒七年二月十三日欽奉寄諭：吳幫辦吉林一切事宜，所有該省辦防及地方諸務均屬責有攸歸，務須往來查察，嚴加督率，不得稍涉諉卸。銘、喜、吳尤當遇事熟商，和衷共濟，毋許各分畛域。等因。欽此。當經恭錄咨會在案。所有一切事宜因值貴幫辦在請假期內，是以未經咨商。茲准大咨，業已奏請銷假，並將應辦事宜應否會銜之處請旨遵行。本將軍自應俟奉到諭旨再行欽遵商辦，相應備文咨覆，為此合咨貴幫辦，請煩查照施行。須至咨者。

右咨欽命幫辦吉林邊務事宜三品卿銜吳。

光緒七年二月。

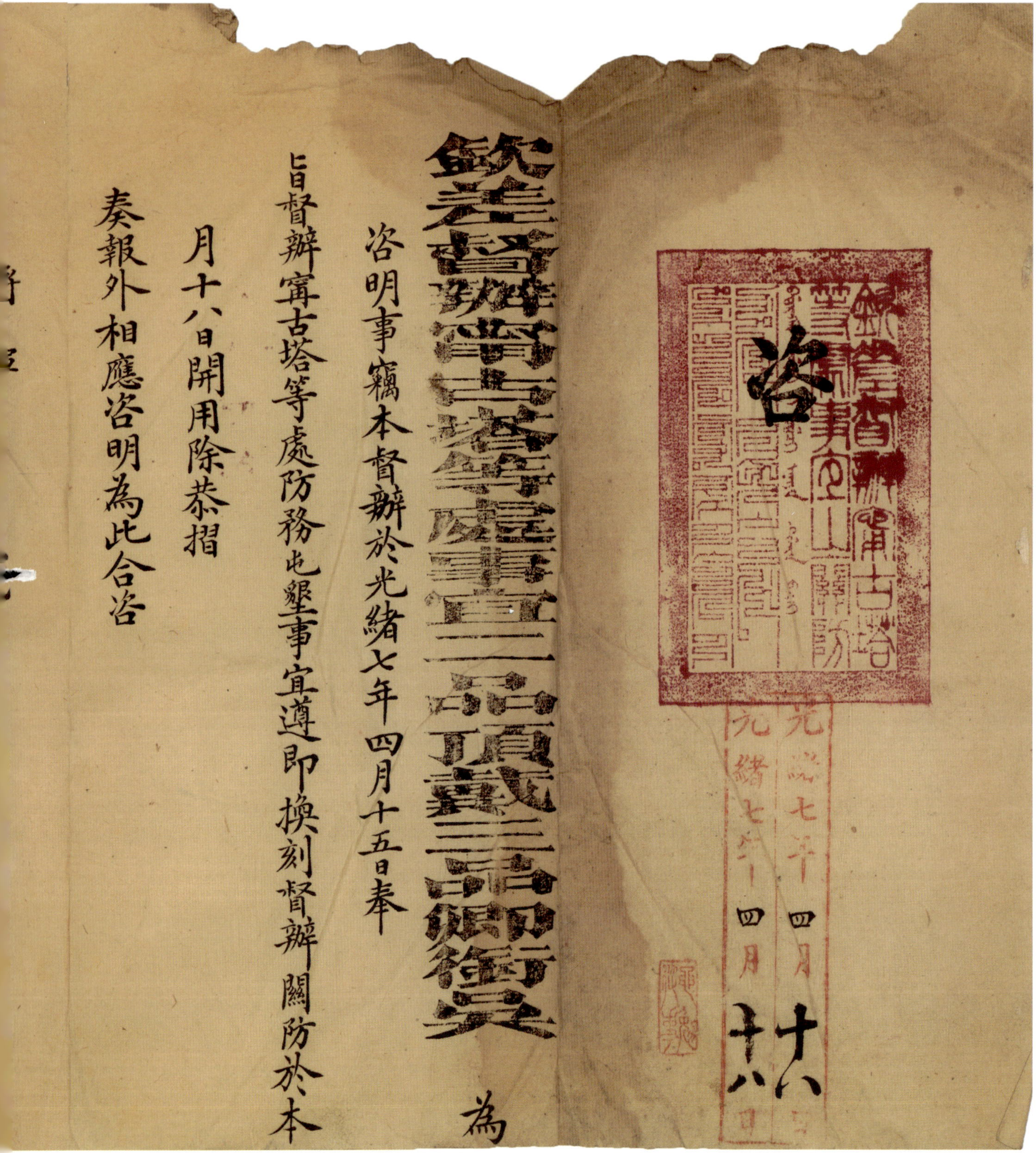
欽差督辦寧古塔等處事宜三品頂戴三品卿銜吳 為
咨明事竊本督辦於光緒七年四月十五日奉
旨督辦寧古塔等處防務屯墾事宜遵即換刻督辦 關防於本
月十八日開用除恭摺
奏報外相應咨明為此合咨

光緒七年（1881年）四月，欽差督辦寧古塔等處事宜吳大澂為奉旨督辦寧古塔等處防務屯墾事宜遵即換刻關防並開用事給吉林將軍的咨

云冈大画

黑白胶片摄影

Yungang in Large Format

Black & White Film Photography

云冈研究院
三晋出版社 编

三晋出版社

《云冈大画幅——黑白胶片摄影》
Yungang in Large Format Black & White Film Photography

《增一阿含经》云，佛为波斯匿王解梦曰：

"梦澄水四边清、中央浊者，当来众生非法欲行，常怀贪嫉，与邪法相应，中国众生好喜斗乱，边国人民无有诤讼也。……当来末世，法应如此。"

按《增一阿含经》，384 年译于前秦长安；"中国"者，释迦牟尼生活的中印度之谓；波斯匿王请佛解梦故事，大约诞生于公元后的贵霜王朝。该故事虽系假托，却真实反映了当时中印度婆罗门教（印度教前身）依然强势，而佛法转往周边地区的历史现状，并准确预言了世界佛教发展的趋向。大致而言，从佛陀涅槃五百年开始，印度佛教在异国他壤茁壮成长，不断掀起一个又一个高潮，创造出一次又一次的辉煌。在遥远的东方，公元五世纪北魏首都平城（今山西大同）佛教的兴盛与云冈石窟的开凿，便是西来像法在华夏大地奏响的一曲惊世乐章。

一
佛教东传的波浪式轨迹

释迦牟尼的生前死后，佛教主要传播于印度的恒河中游一带。公元前三世纪中叶，摩揭陀国孔雀王朝阿育王在统一印度的战争中，因杀戮过多，心生忏悔而皈依佛门。他巡礼佛迹，颁布敕令，广建塔寺，开凿石窟，并在华氏城（今印度比哈尔邦的巴特那）举行了第三次佛典结集，印度佛教盛极一时。当时阿育王派遣出国传教僧侣的足迹，北达辛头河（今印度河）上游，南至师子国（今斯里兰卡）海岛。以帕米尔高原为中心的中亚山区，地扼东西交通要冲，既是印度河、阿姆河、锡尔河、塔里木河等大河的发源地，又是古代印度、波斯、中华、希腊、罗马等世界各大文明的交汇之所。在今天印度河上游的克什米尔、巴基斯坦、阿富汗的山间谷地，曾经沐浴古印度文明的曙光；公元前四世纪末，马其顿国王亚历山大东征后，希腊文化又在这里生根发芽。阿育王所遣沙门宣讲的佛传故事，在感化北印度居民的同时，也激发了犍陀罗（今巴基斯坦白沙瓦）、罽宾（即迦湿弥罗，今克什米尔）等地信众对佛陀神话与形象的新思维。

公元一世纪中叶，来自中国西北、君临大夏（希腊·巴克特里亚帝国，今阿姆河上游）二百年的大月氏民族进一步强盛，建立了贵霜帝国，并在第三代国王迦腻色迦时达到鼎盛，向南迁都犍陀罗，疆域扩大至印度河与恒河流域。迦腻色迦是继阿育王之后，极力推广佛教的又一位国王。在他的支持下，佛教僧侣于迦湿弥罗城举行第四次佛藏结集，罽宾遂为大乘佛教的发源地。大乘佛学是以纯粹佛说参合犍陀罗、罽宾、乌苌国等地传说与魔术，连同希腊、罗马神像解释组成的一种超越恒河沿岸原始佛教的神学。为了取信于人，他们在北印度创建出许多佛迹：中印度有四大塔，北印度亦有四大塔；伽耶城有佛影，那竭城亦有佛影；那竭国界醯罗城有佛顶骨，弗楼沙国有佛钵（见《佛国记》《大唐西域记》）。同时，编造出如来降服恶龙、舍身饲虎、舍头施人、挑眼施鹰、割肉贸鸽、王射睒子等众多本生故事及发生地（见《佛国记》《宋云行记》）。迦腻色迦王振兴佛法的愿望与行动，使犍陀罗变成了恒河流域之外的第二个佛教圣地。

大乘佛教在犍陀罗的流行，一改自阿育王以来，用宝座、脚印、圣树、佛塔、石柱、莲花、大象、雄狮、鹿等形象暗喻佛主的传统，首次允许将佛陀绘画、雕塑为人形，从而宣布了佛教像法时期的来临。这时，大量的佛陀、弥勒、本生故事都用当地一种青灰色片岩雕刻，也用灰泥、石膏制作雕塑和浮雕。佛陀神态矜持，拥有令人喜爱的阿波罗型面容，或立或坐，始终穿着轻柔的内衣和僧袍。菩萨身上佩带着各种珠宝饰物，脚穿雅典式的缀宝凉鞋，与佛陀区别开来。以希腊化为特征的犍陀罗佛教艺术走向鼎盛。在贵霜王朝统治下的恒河流域，受犍陀罗的影响，秣菟罗艺术创造出大量精美的红、黄砂岩佛教雕像。佛陀如沙门，身体壮硕；菩萨戴宝冠，略带微笑。到四世纪后的印度笈多王朝，上述两种艺术进一步融合，突出表现为湿衣贴体和双目低垂的笈多式佛像艺术。

新疆是佛教东传的第一站。印度僧侣越过葱岭，最初进入新疆，应在公元之前。迦腻色迦时代，佛陀的教法在北印度放射出的万丈光芒，首先照亮了整个中亚山川，佛法东传势力转强。从东汉明帝时洛阳白马寺僧摄摩腾、竺法兰翻译的《四十二章经》小乘教义，到安世高小乘禅学、支谶与竺佛朔大乘禅观的输入，一世纪至二世纪中华佛教秉承西学的史迹确凿；从朱士行西天取经，到鸠摩罗什、法显传记所展现的西域诸国，三世纪至四世纪新疆佛教如日中天。尽管现在我们对佛教征服新疆的步伐并非清晰，但新疆佛法早于汉地，无可置疑。大约先是小乘佛教遍行南疆，然后才是大乘佛学的异军突起。当此之时，龟兹（今库车）、焉耆、鄯善（今若羌）、且末等国俱行小乘，于阗（今和田）、子合（今叶城）、沙勒（即疏勒，今喀什）等国多有大乘。兴建塔寺、营造石窟、顶戴佛钵（在沙勒）、讲经说法、行像散华，呈现出一派佛土庄严。犍陀罗佛教艺术的源源而至，拉升了新疆各城邦文化繁荣。由于当地石材的缺乏，泥塑、壁画、木雕构筑起新疆艺术大厦。新疆佛教的昌盛，成为引领汉地佛教走向辉煌的灯塔。

中华佛教始传于东汉，酝酿于魏晋，勃兴于十六国，鼎盛于南北朝，成熟于隋唐，复兴于宋辽金元，衰落于明清。其间，十六国、南北朝是关键。佛教西来的途径有二：西南海路与西北陆路。然以丝绸之路为主线。如果说公元前后大月氏、贵霜的僧人东游弘法，走的是一条回乡之路的话，那么四世纪以后佛教在中华大地上开花结果，实得益于五胡十六国民族大迁徙的历史机缘。

东汉时期，佛教虽传中土，但朝廷以其西戎之神，唯听西域人立寺都邑，汉人皆不得出家。魏晋以后，法禁渐弛。西晋末年，天下大乱，来自华夏西、北的匈奴、鲜卑、羯、氐、羌等少数民族纷纷建立政权，逐鹿中原。佛教作为胡教，不但被各胡族统治者立为国教，以"助王政之禁律，益仁智之善性"（《魏书·释老志》，下引该志不再注明），而且成为颠沛流离、苦难深重的华夷百姓维生系命的精神依托。首先提倡佛教的是后赵羯族皇帝石勒、石虎，他们敬奉西域高僧佛图澄为大和尚，广建伽蓝，说法授徒，参咨国政。石虎公然宣称："朕生自边壤，君临诸夏；佛是戎神，正所应奉。其夷、赵百姓，有舍其淫祀，乐事佛者，悉听为道。""于是中州胡、晋略皆奉佛"（《高僧传·竺佛图澄》）。中原佛教迎来了第一次短暂的高潮，佛陀救世思想深入人心。随后的前秦氐族皇帝苻坚、后秦羌族皇帝姚兴相继崇法，释道安、鸠摩罗什、佛驮跋陀罗等大师辈出，译经讲论，立戒修禅，一时间长安成为中夏佛教的中心。大约同时，西秦乞伏氏政权与北凉沮渠氏政权，亦将陇右、河西佛法推向高峰。佛教信仰成为中国社会不可逆转的时代潮流。

北魏王朝的建立者拓跋鲜卑，族源来自大兴安岭深处，东汉后期游牧塞北，魏晋之时部落始大。在五胡争霸之余，拓跋鲜卑担负起收拾中原残局的历史使命。398 年，道武帝拓跋珪定都平城，建立北魏；439 年，太武帝拓跋焘统一中国北方；448 年，征服西域（今新疆）；494 年，孝文帝拓跋宏迁都洛阳；534 年，北魏分裂为东魏、西魏。不久，分别被北齐、北周取代。拓跋鲜卑原本不知有佛，然从平城到洛阳，却因礼佛近乎痴狂，所以北齐魏收撰《魏书》，独创《释老志》以述其事云："魏有天下，至于禅让，佛经流通，大集中国，凡有四百一十五部，合一千九百一十九卷。正光已后，天下多虞，王役尤甚，于是所在编民，相与入道，假慕沙门，实避调役，猥滥之极，自中国之有佛法，未之有也。略而计之，僧尼大众二百万矣，其寺三万有余。流弊不归，一至于此，识者所以叹息也。"与此同时，江南的梁武帝萧衍也因佞佛身丧国亡，留给后人"南朝四百八十寺，多少楼台烟雨中"之类的伤感。中华佛教盛极而悲。

二
云冈石窟开凿的历史因缘

云冈石窟位于大同城西 16 千米的武州山南麓，武州川（今十里河）北岸。北魏旧称武州山石窟寺或代京灵岩寺。石窟倚山开凿，东西绵延约 1 千米。现存大小窟龛 254 个，主要洞窟 45 座，造像 59000 余尊。石窟规模宏大，造像内容丰富，雕刻艺术精湛，形象生动感人，堪称中华佛教艺术的巅峰之作，代表了五世纪世界美术雕刻的最高水平。

关于云冈石窟的开凿，《释老志》记述如下：“和平初，师贤卒。昙曜代之，更名‘沙门统’。初，昙曜以复佛法之明年，自中山被命赴京，值帝出，见于路，御马前衔曜衣，时以为马识善人。帝後奉以师礼。昙曜白帝，于京城西武州塞，凿山石壁，开窟五所，镌建佛像各一。高者七十尺，次六十尺，雕饰奇伟，冠于一世。”文中提及的武州塞，位于云冈石窟西崖之北，赵武灵王以来一直是由蒙古高原进入汉地的交通要塞。武州山的砂岩，是西来佛徒熟悉的雕刻石材。昙曜建议开凿的五所佛窟，即今云冈第16至20窟，学者谓之“昙曜五窟”。周一良《云冈石佛小记》曰：“惟昙曜在兴安二年见帝后即开窟，抑为沙门统之后始建斯议？不可晓。要之，石窟之始开也，在兴安二年（453）至和平元年（460）之八年间。”

昙曜五窟的开凿，掀起了武州山石窟寺建设的热潮。从文成帝开始，经献文帝、冯太后，到孝文帝迁都，皇家经营约四十年，完成了所有大窟大像的开凿。同时，云冈附近的鹿野苑石窟、青磁窑石窟、鲁班窑石窟、吴官屯石窟、焦山寺石窟等也相继完成。期间，广泛吸收民间资金，王公大臣、各地官吏、善男信女纷纷以个人、家族、邑社等形式参与石窟建造，或建一窟，或造一壁，或捐一龛，或施一躯，遂成就了武州山石窟寺的蔚然大观。迁都之后，武州山石窟建设仍延续了三十年，直到正光五年（524）六镇起义的战鼓响起。

云冈石窟的诞生并非偶然，它是诸多历史必然性的归结。

第一，礼帝为佛的新思维，是引领北魏佛教兴盛的法宝。道武帝建都平城，“始作五级佛图、耆阇崛山及须弥山殿，加以绘饰。别构讲堂、禅堂及沙门座，莫不严具焉。”约此同时，任命赵郡（今河北赵县）高僧法果为道人统，绾摄僧徒。“法果每言，太祖明叡好道，即是当今如来，沙门宜应尽礼，遂常致拜。谓人曰：‘能鸿道者人主也，我非拜天子，乃是礼佛耳。’”在此之前，西域胡僧入华，奉敬其佛，无须礼拜皇帝，而东晋十六国以后，出家汉人成为主流，原本是天子的臣民，现在变为释迦门徒，因此沙门拜不拜皇帝，即是否承认和接受国家管理，成为南北佛教必须回答的问题。对此，隐居庐山的慧远和尚著有《沙门不敬王者论》，代表了南方释子的立场；法果的言行，则表明了北方僧人的态度。同为佛图澄的再传弟子，他俩选择的方式截然相反，南北佛教所走的路也明显不同。法果所言，虽涉阿谀，又似诡辩，汲取的却是佛图澄依国弘法、以术干政的成功经验，遵循的竟是释道安“不依国主，则法事难立”名训。盖佛教离不开人主，人主也需要神化。法果将帝佛合一，提出皇帝就是当今如来（活佛）的新理论，巧妙地将释迦信徒转回到天子门下，迎合了最高统治者的心理需求，使宗教行为上升为国家意志，从而奠定了北朝佛教鼎盛的基础。后来的北魏僧统师贤为文成帝立像“令如帝身”，昙曜在武州山为五位皇祖开窟造像，实属法果理论的再创造和付诸实施。武州山石窟寺因此列入皇家工程，成为几代皇帝建造家庙的自觉行动。

第二，平城佛教中心的形成，使大规模像教建设成为可能。从道武帝建国，到太武帝结束北方群雄割据的局面，北魏推行的掠夺与徙民政策，使平城这座昔日的边陲小县迅速跃升为北中国政治、军事、经济和文化中心。随后对西域的征服，又将平城推向东方国际大都市的新高峰。在各国各地贵族官僚、儒道沙门、能工巧匠、租赋商贩、金银财富汇聚平城的同时，佛教信仰也日益升温。特别是北魏太延五年（439）灭北凉，《释老志》称：“凉州自张轨后，世信佛教。敦煌地接西域，道俗交得其旧式，村坞相属，多有塔寺。太延中，凉州平，徙其国人于京邑，沙门佛事皆俱东，象教弥增矣。”凉州（治姑臧，今甘肃武威）所辖河西走廊，自古是中西文化交融之地，也是西域胡僧进入中土的第一站。四世纪初，张轨任凉州刺史，河西奉佛已成民风。417年，东晋大将刘裕攻灭姚氏后秦，长安僧众四散奔逃，河西佛教遂为中华一枝独秀。太武帝徙凉州吏民三万户（包括参与守城被俘的三千僧人）于京城，如同河西佛教整体“搬迁”，平城随即成为中华佛教的新中心。曾经目睹天竺、西域佛事，参与敦煌莫高窟、武威天梯山、永靖炳灵寺、天水麦积山等河陇石窟开凿、禅修的凉州僧匠，成为未来平城佛寺与石窟寺建设的主力。

第三，太武帝灭佛，从反方向刺激了北魏佛教的迅猛发展。凉州僧团的东迁，在促成平城佛教骤盛的同时，也引发了中国历史上第一次佛道之争。受嵩山道士寇谦之、司徒崔浩的影响，太武帝于真君七年（446）诏令灭法。一时间，北魏民间“金银宝像及诸经论，大得秘藏。而土木宫塔，声教所及，莫不毕毁矣。”然而，毁之愈烈，求之弥切。兴安元年（452），文成帝拓跋濬即位甫尔，在群臣的请求下，宣令复法。“方诏遣立像，其徒惟恐再毁，谓木有时朽，土有时崩，金有时烁，至覆石以室，可永无忧。又虑像小可凿而去，径尺不已，至数尺，数尺不已，必穷其力至数十尺。累数百千，而佛乃久存不坏，使见者因像生感。”（朱彝尊《云冈石佛记》）。于是乎，昙曜五佛应运而出。

第四，追仿释迦鹿苑旧事，再造东方佛教圣地。鹿苑，即鹿野苑，释迦牟尼“初转法轮”的说法成道处，在今印度贝拿勒斯城郊。北魏鹿苑，在平城皇宫北，道武帝天兴二年（399）起筑，“东包白登，属之西山”（《魏书·高车传》）。苑之西山，道武帝拓跋珪时，封山禁樵；明元帝拓跋嗣时，奉武州山为神山筑坛祭祀；太武帝平定凉州以后，逐渐成为西来沙门采石雕佛开窟修禅之所。于是平城鹿苑与印度鹿苑，在凉州僧众的心目中自然成双，产生共鸣。特别是昙曜五佛的横空出世，极大地鼓舞了年轻的献文帝拓跋弘，坚定了他追仿西天胜迹，建立东方鹿野苑的信心。高允《鹿苑赋》云：“暨我皇之继统，诞天纵之明叡；追鹿野之在昔，兴三转之高义；振幽宗于已永，旷千载而有寄。于是命匠选工，刊兹西岭；注诚端思，仰模神影；庶真容之仿佛，耀金晖之焕炳。即灵崖以构宇，疏百寻而直上；絙飞梁于浮柱，列荷华于绮井。图之以万形，缀之以清永；若祇洹之瞪对，孰道场之途迥。嗟神功之所建，超终古而秀出。”武州山石窟寺建设全面展开。

第五，西风东渐，共铸辉煌。北魏对西域的征服，直接迎来了我国历史上第二次东西文化交流的高潮。作为丝绸之路东端的大都会，平城迅速成为胡商梵僧云集之地。印度石窟造像之风，经由新疆，波及河西、关陇，至平城而特盛，进而流布中华。武州山石窟的创作，最初是凉州僧匠带来了西域风格的佛教造像艺术，然后是古印度、师子国西域诸国的胡沙门带着佛经、佛像和画本，随商队、使团而至，再后是昙曜建议征集全国各地的宝像于京师，最后是徐州僧匠北上主持云冈佛事。一代代、一批批的高僧大德、艺匠精工，共同设计、共同制作，创造出云冈石窟一座座旷世无双的佛国天堂。

作为新疆以东最早出现的大型石窟群，武州山石窟寺的壮丽与辉煌，在震惊当世的同时，成为引领和推动北朝石窟佛寺建设高潮的样板。由云冈向东的辽宁义县万佛堂石窟，向南的洛阳龙门石窟、巩县石窟、山西太原天龙山石窟、河北邯郸响堂山石窟等，向西的甘肃泾川南石窟寺、庆阳北石窟寺、天水麦积山石窟寺、永靖炳灵寺、敦煌莫高窟等，无不受其影响。从北魏昙曜开窟至初唐道宣遥礼，近二百年间，无论政治风云如何变幻，代京灵岩始终是中华僧徒心中的圣地。云冈石窟的开凿对华夏石窟寺的推广、雕刻艺术的发展，产生了深远的影响。

三

东方佛教艺术的旷世绝唱

关于云冈石窟的艺术源流，一百多年来中外学者论述颇丰：有埃及影响说、希腊影响说、拓跋氏影响说，还有犍陀罗艺术、秣菟罗艺术、笈多艺术、西域（新疆）艺术输入说等。其中，以犍陀罗艺术、秣菟罗成分、新疆风格等观点最为流行。北魏文成帝“太安初，有师子国胡沙门邪奢遗多、浮陀难提等五人，奉佛像三到京都。皆云，备历西域诸国，见佛影迹及肉髻，外国诸王相承，咸遣工匠，摹写其容，莫能及难提所造者，去十余步，视之炳然，转近转微。又沙勒胡沙门，赴京师致佛钵并画像迹”。上述记载表明，平城、云冈佛像与印度、新疆艺术有着一定的传承关系。然而，考察犍陀罗、秣菟罗佛教造像，我们总会产生一种似是而非的困惑，因为实在找不到多少与云冈石窟完全相同的东西。而那些造型、气韵、时尚方面的差异，显然表明彼此之间文化、艺术关系的断裂，或存有阙环。相反，对新疆早期佛教遗存的观摩，则令我们倍感熟悉和亲切。

这种亲近的感受，来自库车克孜尔石窟，也来自新疆遗存的中心方塔式佛殿，更来自塔里木盆地南北那种拓制便利、样式纷繁、面如满月、充满异国情调的黄泥塑像。

从佛法东传的时代背景分析，凉州僧匠最初带到平城的只能是凉州模式或西域样式，而凉州模式实际上就是西域南北两道佛教的混合艺术。新疆式的犍陀罗艺术甚至秣菟罗艺术，移花接木般地在云冈石窟翻版，应当属于历史的必然。尤其是大乘佛教盛行的于阗、子合等地像法。从云冈石窟的工程本身分析，凉州僧匠是规划设计的主体，其所依凭的佛像、画本及其造像法则，无论直接还是间接模仿西域，设计蓝图必定是经过北魏皇帝、有司会审批准的，鲜卑与汉民族的审美愿望自然渗透其中。开凿洞窟的工匠，包括部分凉州僧人，但主体是来自中原各地的汉人，因而大量运用的是中国传统的雕刻技艺和表达方式。我们讲，西式设计与中式技艺是云冈最大特点。当然，越往后来，中华传统的份量越重，自主创新的意识越强。这就是为什么云冈造像艺术并不简单雷同于印度、中亚、新疆的原因。

作为西来像法在中华大地绽放出的第一朵奇葩，云冈石窟一改葱岭以东石窟寺泥塑、壁画、木雕为主的艺术模式，直接比照印度的大型石窟建筑，在东方首次营造出气势磅礴的全石雕性质的佛教石窟群；同时，广泛吸收中外造像艺术精华，兼容并蓄，融会贯通，成为中国早期佛教艺术的集大成者。云冈石窟开凿大致分为三期，即三个阶段。早期为文成帝时昙曜五窟的开凿，中期为献文帝、冯太后、孝文帝时皇家营造的大窟大像，晚期为迁洛后民间补刻的窟龛。云冈造像分为两类：前则西域风格，后则华夏新式。集中展现了西来像法逐步中国化、世俗化的演进过程，堪称中华佛教艺术发展的里程碑。

昙曜五佛是云冈石窟的典型代表，也是西域造像艺术东传的顶级作品。大佛身着的袈裟，或披或袒，衣纹厚重，似属毛纺织品，这无疑是中亚山间牧区国家的服装特征。大佛具高肉髻，方额丰颐，高鼻深目，眉眼细长，嘴角上翘，大耳垂肩，身躯挺拔、健硕，神情庄严而又和蔼可亲，气度恢宏。诚如唐代道宣大师所云："造像梵相，宋、齐间，皆唇厚、鼻隆、目长、颐丰，挺然丈夫之相。"（宋《释氏要览》卷二）特别是第 20 窟的露天大佛，法相庄严，气宇轩昂，充满活力，将拓跋鲜卑的剽悍与强大、粗犷与豪放、宽宏与睿智的民族精神表现得淋漓尽致、出神入化，给人以心灵的震撼。而第 18 窟主尊大佛东侧的十位弟子，相貌、神态各异，均为西方人种，具有显著的西域特征。

献文帝继位（466 年）后，对武州山石窟工程进行了重新部署，建设规模扩大化、洞窟形制多样化、图像内容多元化的步伐加快。迄孝文帝太和十八年（494）迁都洛阳，云冈石窟的建设达到鼎盛。这一时期开凿完成的洞窟，有第 1、2 窟，第 5、6 窟四组双窟，第 7、8 窟，第 9、10 窟和第 11、12、13 窟一组三窟，以及未完工的第 3 窟。在洞窟形制上，不仅有穹隆型，还出现了方形中心塔柱窟，以及前后殿堂式洞窟。在佛龛造型上，不仅有圆拱龛、盝形龛、宝盖龛，又增加了屋形龛、帷幕龛和复合形龛等。平面方形洞窟的大量出现，较早期穹隆型洞窟而言，雕刻面积大幅度增加，雕刻内容与形式也变得复杂起来。洞窟的顶部，多采用平棊藻井式雕刻；壁面的雕刻，采取了上下重层、左右分段的方式。这一时期的造像题材，虽仍以释迦、弥勒为主，但雕刻内容不断增加，依凭的佛经明显增多，普遍流行的是释迦说法或禅定龛像、释迦与多宝并坐龛式、七佛造型、维摩与文殊问答图像，以及着菩萨装或佛装的交脚菩萨龛式等。护法天神像，开始雕刻在门拱两侧；佛本生、佛本行故事龛和连幅画，出现在列壁最直观的位置；作为出资者的供养人形象，以左右对称排列的形式出现在壁龛的下方；佛塔、廊柱、庑殿等建筑造型跃然而出；飞天、比丘、力士、金刚、伎乐天、供养天千姿百态；各种动物、花纹图案争奇斗妍。至此，云冈艺术宝库的真容毕具。

第 7、8 窟是云冈营造最早的双窟，窟顶用莲花与飞天装饰的平棊藻井，赋予中国传统建筑样式以佛国仙境般的浪漫。第 7 窟门拱两侧的三头四臂神像，头戴尖顶帽，极具中、西亚特征。第 8 窟门拱两侧，三头八臂、骑牛的摩醯首罗天，五头六臂、乘鸟的鸠摩罗天，其形象来源于古印度神话中的天神湿婆和毗湿奴，他俩一位可以毁灭宇宙，另一位则能够创造世界。这种将婆罗门教大神转化为佛教护法神的现象，是印度密教思想的反映，完全属于西来像法，为中西石窟寺的绝版遗存。第 9、10 窟是中国传统的殿堂式建筑，但其窟外前庭由雄狮、大象驮起的廊柱和建筑造型，则混合兼备了古印度与希腊、罗马建筑艺术风格；后室门廊两侧头顶羽冠的金刚天王，威武勇猛，是云冈石窟护法像中的典型。第 5、6 窟规模宏大，前者为大像窟，主尊高达 17.4 米，为云冈佛像之最；后者为塔庙窟，设计完整，雕刻纷繁，尤以描述释迦牟尼生平故事的系列浮雕连幅画著称于世。第 12 窟亦为廊柱式殿堂窟，俗称"音乐窟"，其前室北壁上方的伎乐天手持各种东、西方乐器，宛若一支"交响乐团"，是研究我国古代音乐史的珍贵素材。这些富丽堂皇的洞窟建筑，绚丽多彩的石刻艺术，惊世骇俗的伟大创造，是中华民族奉献给全人类的不朽杰作。

云冈石窟的中期建设，受到了北魏社会弥勒信仰和西方净土思想的影响，在竭力营造人间"兜率天宫"的同时，正处于一个继往开来的蓬勃发展阶段。一方面是西来之风不断，胡风胡韵依然浓郁，占据着主导地位；另一方面是中华传统势力抬头，汉式建筑、服饰、雕刻技艺和审美情趣逐渐显露。我们能够感觉到，佛、菩萨等造像的雕凿，主要模仿的是新疆泥塑。那些形象多样的悬挂式低温黄陶影塑，当时已在平城附近大批量生产，并用来装潢佛塔、寺院，同时为云冈雕刻提供了大量鲜活的样本。与早期造像相比，中期造像健硕、美丽依旧，但似乎逐渐丧失了内在的刚毅与个性，雕刻如同拓制泥塑一样程式化了。大像、主像和重要造像的雕琢是精细的，普通性的造像略显草率，工匠洗练的刀法仿佛于漫不经心间流淌出来，反而给人以自由、活泼、奔放的感觉。部分佛像开始变得清秀，面相适中；佛衣除了袒右肩式、通肩式袈裟之外，出现了"褒衣博带"样式。菩萨的衣饰也发生了变化，除头戴宝冠者外，又流行起花蔓冠；身佩璎珞，斜披络腋，转变为身披帔帛；裙衣贴腿，转变为裙裾张扬。这些佛装、菩萨装向着汉族衣冠服饰转化的倾向，显然是太和十年（486）后孝文帝实行服制改革、推行汉化政策的反映。由此，填补了我国南北朝佛教艺术从"胡貌梵相"到"改梵为夏"的演变过程的空白。

在云冈石窟中，汉民族意识的觉醒，我们说不清经历了多长时间。但是，深受西域佛教、像法影响的凉州僧团的领导地位，大约从太和五年（481）开始动摇了。随后，徐州义学高僧接受了孝文帝的邀请，率徒北上，"唱谛鹿苑，作匠京缁"（《广弘明集·元魏孝文帝为慧纪法师亡施帛设斋诏》），代京平城的佛学风气为之一变。到太和十三年（489），褒衣博带、秀骨清像登上了云冈第 11 窟外壁的佛龛，并从此成为时尚。如果说云冈第 6 窟中最早出现的褒衣博带式佛像，尚未脱离"胡貌梵相"，那么第 11、12、13 窟外壁众多龛洞的造像则是完全"改梵为夏"了。

孝文帝迁都洛阳后，平城依然为北都，云冈的皇家工程基本结束，但民间盛行的开窟造像之风犹烈。尽管大窟减少，但中小窟龛却自东迄西遍布崖面。这些数量众多的晚期洞窟，类型复杂，式样多变，但洞窟内部却日益方整。塔窟、四壁三龛及重龛式的洞窟，是这一时期流行的窟式。造像内容题材，趋于模式化、简单化。佛像一律褒衣博带，面容消瘦，细颈削肩，神情显得飘渺虚无；菩萨身材修长，帔帛交叉，表情孤傲，给人以清秀俊逸、超凡脱俗的感觉，显然符合了中国人心目中对神仙形象的理解。造像衣服下部的褶纹越来越重叠，龛楣、帐饰日益繁杂，窟外崖面的雕饰也越来越繁缛。上述风格与特征，与龙门石窟的北魏造像同出一辙，标志着中华民族对西来佛教像法的引进与吸收过程的初步终结。

四

平城时代对中国佛教的重大贡献

北魏定都平城的 97 年，是中国佛教成长壮大、方兴未艾的关键时期。除了云冈石窟对于后世石窟建设、美术发展的影响之外，此间引进、形成、确立、巩固的佛学思想，以及僧官体制、僧尼制度及寺院经济模式，对后世佛教发展影响深远。

（一）

佛教为统治者服务思想的确立。汤用彤《汉魏两晋南北朝佛教史》讲："盖释迦在世，波斯匿王信奉三宝，经卷传为美谈。其后孔雀朝之阿输迦，贵霜朝之迦腻色迦，光大教化，释子推为盛事。"可见，佛教与政治联姻由来已久。《付法藏因缘传》记迦那提婆在南天竺传教时讲："树不伐本，枝条难倾；人主不化，道岂流布？"这种依靠国王弘扬佛法的思想，远早于释道安"不依国主，则法事难立"的感悟，应属佛教传统。然而，佛教传入中华，汉魏以来有明确的法令限制，汉人不得为僧，朝廷不礼胡神。因此那些随商旅而至的胡沙门，只能以江湖医巫、打卦算命、祭神祈雨等方式，在民间缓慢传播；佛教只能隐没其助国兴善的大智略，依托黄老、玄学而后行。这样形同方术、潜移默化的过程，持续了三个多世纪，直到后赵石氏率先奉佛。佛图澄是促成佛教与中原政权结合的第一人，《高僧传》云："受业追游，常有数百，前后门徒，几且一万。所历州郡，兴立佛寺八百九十三所。弘法之盛，莫与先矣。"后赵虽系短命王朝，中土佛教信仰却从此蔚然成风。北魏法果在佛图澄死后三十余年入道，其师承何人不详，但传习的不外乎佛图澄教法。法果礼帝为佛的弘法思想，祖承佛图澄经验，契合释道安名训，明确了佛教为最高统治者服务的方针。所以，后来文成帝在复法诏书中，对如来功德予以充分肯定："助王政之禁律，益仁智之善性，排斥群邪，开演正觉。"佛教因此被纳入封建政治，成为中华王朝始终奉行的统治术之一。其帝佛合一思想，亦为后世佞佛帝王所因袭，武则天自谓弥勒下生，广树大像；明武宗自称"大庆法王西天觉道圆明自在大定慧佛"，可谓一脉相承。

（二）

僧官制度的形成与《僧制》的颁行。北魏道武帝任命法果"为道人统，绾摄僧徒"，是正史记载佛教设官之始，标志着中华佛教走出低迷，从此步入上层建筑。文成帝和平初年（460），改道人统为沙门统。大约当时由于京城僧侣既多，又设都维那，作为沙门都统之副贰。另外，在朝廷设立监福曹，管理全国佛教事务；在州镇、畿郡亦设僧统、维那，管辖属地僧尼。其寺院仿效西域故事，设立维那、上座、寺主，所谓三纲。孝文帝时，受太和五年法秀谋反的影响，一方面加强僧籍管理，限制僧人游方，禁止私度僧尼；另一方面改监福曹为昭玄，备有官属，以断僧务。特别太和十七年，"诏立《僧制》四十七条"，从法律上宣告了中国僧尼制度的诞生。这是迄今我们知晓的第一部国家颁行的僧尼法典，既不同于古印度阿育王石柱敕令，也不同于释迦牟尼以来天竺僧团自行规定的戒律（传至中华有五部律）。一则表明僧尼作为一个特殊的社会群体，正式获得了国家的承认；二则表明这种承认是有条件的，必须服从国家法律。"世宗即位，永平元年秋，诏曰：缁素既殊，法律亦异。……自今已后，众僧犯杀人已上罪者，仍依俗断，余犯悉付昭玄，以内律、《僧制》治之。"可见，北魏僧尼外遵国典，内奉戒律、僧制，享有一定的独立权利。北魏平城时代确立的僧官、僧制模式，尽管今天我们尚未完全明晰，但其作为隋唐制度的渊源没有疑义。

（三）

寺院经济的诞生与独立发展。印度佛教僧侣最初的生活方式，主要是沿街乞食与信徒施舍。大约后来随佛教影响力的增长，寺院逐渐拥有了自己的依附人口和固定的经济收入。北魏太武帝平凉州，僧众被俘、迁徙于京师，生活必定经历了一段艰难困苦时期。迨文成复法，京邑、地方纷纷造寺度僧，特别是武州山等石窟寺的开凿，集中了大批的僧侣、工匠。如何解决僧人用粮、寺院用工，自然成为沙门统昙曜必须从长计议的问题。于是"昙曜奏：平齐户及诸民，有能岁输谷六十斛入僧曹者，即为'僧祇户'，粟为'僧祇粟'，至于俭岁，赈给饥民。又请民犯重罪及官奴以为'佛图户'，以供诸寺扫洒，岁兼营田输粟。高宗并许之。于是僧祇户、粟及寺户，遍于州镇矣"。按：僧祇，即僧尼大众；僧祇户，乃依附于僧众的人户；僧祇粟，即供养僧众的粟米。佛图户，即寺户，是专为佛寺僧众提供杂役的奴婢，如同西域佛寺中的净人。佛图户与僧祇户、粟的出现，保障了北魏沙门佛事之需，是中国寺院经济形成与独立的标志。到唐代，寺院、道观依然有两种贱民，一曰部曲，二曰奴婢，与北魏异名而同趣。这种新兴的寺院经济，凭仗着政治、经济上的治外法权，从此成为中国地主庄园经济的一种特殊形式，与封建社会相始终。

（四）

僧团政治核心的形成与传承。魏晋特别是南北朝时期，中国佛教渐趋成熟，无论是经、律、论三藏之学，还是僧尼的政治、经济地位，都处于上升阶段。北方重禅业，南方尚讲经，弘法的方式虽有差异，但分别教派、扩张力量、追逐名利的情形却是相同的。北魏太和中，坐禅的凉州僧与讲经的徐州僧在平城相遇，可以说是南北佛教势力首次大规模的交锋。尽管我们现在对其详情不甚明了，但完全可以想见徐州高僧的后来者居上，对凉州旧僧形成的压力及其失落之感。学术之异，政治之争，必然导致双方的严重对立，矛盾与冲突在所难免。这场斗争，从平城开始，以凉州系与徐州系划分；迁都洛阳之后，以禅僧与讲僧区别，一直延续至隋唐不息。《洛阳伽蓝记》卷二载有一则故事：孝昌元年（525），崇真寺比丘惠凝死而复活，讲述他在阎罗王处，看到阎王判禅诵僧升天堂，讲经僧入黑门地狱。灵太后闻知后，"即请坐禅僧一百人常在殿内供养之。……自此以后，京邑比丘悉皆禅诵，不复以讲经为意"。按：惠凝之说，盖系坐禅派僧徒编造，以攻击在政治上占有优势的讲经派僧徒。这无疑是孝文帝时代凉州僧团与徐州僧团斗争的继续。大体而言，从北魏到隋唐，虽政权屡经更迭，但统治主体始终为代北子孙和中原世族；佛教僧团虽互有消长，但上流师德依然应是凉州、徐州系统法脉。

（五）

武州山石窟寺译经与《付法藏因缘传》。十六国南北朝是佛经入华的第一高峰，长安、凉州、建康、平城、洛阳等都城三宝兴隆，译经先后不断。《释老志》曰："昙曜又与天竺沙门常那邪舍等，译出新经十四部。"据隋费长房《历代三宝记》等书记载，自文成帝和平三年（462）至孝文帝太和十年（486），沙门统昙曜于北台石窟寺集诸僧众翻译经论，有《净度三昧经》《付法藏因缘传》《提谓波利经》《杂宝藏经》《大方广菩萨十地经》《方便心经》《大吉义咒经》《佛说称扬诸佛功德经》等。其中，以昙曜与西域三藏吉迦夜共译的《付法藏因缘传》最具影响。该传全面讲述了印度佛教的弘法历程，首次开列出释迦、迦叶、阿难、商那和修、优波毱多、提多迦、弥遮迦、佛陀难提、佛陀蜜多、胁比丘、富那奢、马鸣、比罗、龙树、迦那提婆、罗睺罗、僧伽难提、僧伽耶舍、鸠摩罗驮、阇夜多、婆修槃陀、摩奴罗、鹤勒那、夜奢、师子等印度佛祖传法世系。日本学者关野贞、常盘大定《山西云冈》（赵一德译）中讲："昙曜的付法藏精神，由隋代的灵裕完整地继承下来，灵裕开的宝山石窟，在其内壁刻有世尊寂灭后传法圣师二十四祖像，就是按《付法藏因缘传》二十四祖刻的，灵裕以后尚有许多继承者。"我们认为，昙曜《付法藏因缘传》的翻译，开启了中国佛教祖师传灯思想的先河，唐代以后各佛学宗派盛行的立祖传宗方法渊源于兹。

（六）

《华严经》开始盛行。云冈石窟的开凿，是中国佛教思想体系渐臻完备的反映。关野贞、常盘大定讲："昙曜请求文成帝开凿石窟五所，又是为太祖以下五帝而设，毋庸置疑。这样，五窟就含有五帝的灵庙的意义。……既有昙曜的付法藏精神，也有魏王室忏悔及追孝的动机，这样的因缘凑合，产生了千古的佛教艺术。而造像的指导思想，至少与佛传以及《法华》《维摩》《金光明》《无量寿》《弥勒》等诸大乘经卷有关，华严的思想也是有的。"关于《华严经》在平城的传播情况，《续高僧传》卷二十九记载："太和初年，代京阉官自慨刑余，不逮人族，奏乞入山修道，有敕许之。乃赍一部《华严》，昼夜读诵，礼悔不息。夏首归山，至六月末髭须尽生，复丈夫相，还状奏闻。高祖信敬由来，忽见惊讶，更增常日。于是大代之国《华严》一经，因斯转盛。并见侯君素《旌异记》。"按《华严经》

沙门支法领从于阗携归胡本，420 年天竺禅师佛驮跋陀罗于建康道场寺译出。由于卷部浩大，半个多世纪默默无闻。平城佛教中心形成后，各地僧侣无远而至，《华严》深经的研读、传讲，遂为学术攻关项目，成为热门学问。从此奠定了唐代以降华严宗与华严学兴盛的基础。

（七）

《四分律》的开讲。南北朝时期，中华僧侣奉行的是《僧祇律》。唐道宣《续高僧传》卷二十三论曰："昙无德部《四分》一律，虽翻在姚秦，而创敷元魏。是由赤髭论主初乃诵传，未展谈授，寻还异域。此方学侣，竟绝维持。逮及覆、聪，方开学肆。……今则混一唐统，普行《四分》之宗。……自初开律，释师号法聪，元魏孝文北台扬绪，口以传授，时所荣之。沙门道覆，即绍聪绪，缵疏六卷，但是长科。至于义举，未闻于世。斯时释侣，道味犹淳，言行相承，随闻奉用，专务栖隐，不暇旁求。魏末齐初，慧光宅世，宗匠跋陀，师表弘理，再造文疏，广分衢术。学声学望，连布若云，峰行光德。光荣曜齐日，月每一披阐，坐列千僧，竞鼓清言，人分异辩，勒成卷帙，通号命家。……或传道于东川，或称言于南服。其中高第，无越魏都。"按：赤髭论主，指后秦姚兴时诵出《四分律》的罽宾高僧佛陀耶舍；法聪、道覆，北魏孝文帝时平城律匠；跋陀，天竺僧人，初在平城别设禅林，凿石为龛，后至洛阳，立少林寺；慧光，跋陀之徒。如此说来，《四分律》翻译于后秦长安，始兴于北魏平城，光大于北齐，普行于唐代。平城佛教在律藏方面的贡献，显而易见。

综上所述，北魏平城时代中华佛教中心的形成与确立，在中国佛教史上具有非常重要的里程碑意义，其继往开来的历史地位与作用不可低估。至于平城佛教与艺术对高句丽、日本国的影响，也逐渐为世人所认知。

According to *Ekottaragama-sutra*, the Buddha interpreted a dream for the King Prasenajit, "When you dream about a scene in which the water is clear around but cloudy in the center; when all living beings are greedy, jealousy, and want to do evil and correspond to evil; when natives in the Central Kingdom like to fight against each other while people in the bordering regions have no arguments ... The last phase of the age will come. It is determined by the laws of nature." The *Ekottaragama-sutra* was translated at Chang'an in A.D. 384 of the Former Qin Dynasty. In that sutra, "Central Kingdom" actually means central India of Shakyamuni's time. The story about King Prasenajit asking Buddha to interpret the dream was created in the Kushan Dynasty after the Christian era. Although the story is false, it truly reflects the situation that Brahmanism (Forerunner of Hinduism) was still popular in central India, while Buddhism moved to the bordering areas. It also predicts the development direction of Buddhism in the world. Broadly speaking, five hundred years after the Buddha's nirvana, Indian Buddhism thrived in foreign lands, setting off one climax after another, creating one glory after another. In the remote eastern land, the prosperity of Buddhism and the creation of Yungang Grottoes in Pingcheng (Datong, the present city of Shanxi Province), the capital of the Northern Wei Dynasty in the 5th century A.D., demonstrate a stunning piece of music in the land of China.

A.
The wavy track of eastward Buddhism

Around Shakyamuni's life time, Buddhism mainly spread along the middle section of the Ganges River in India. Asoka, the King of the Mauryan Kingdom of Magadha, felt guilty about too much killing in wars to unify India and converted to Buddhism in the middle of 3rd century B.C. He visited Buddhist sites, promulgated decrees, widely built towers and temples, dug grottoes (Fig.1), and held the 3rd Buddhist assembly for the collection and fixing of the Buddhist canon in Pataliputra (Patna in Bihar, India). Indian Buddhism therefore flourished. At that time, many monks were sent abroad by Asoka to spread Buddhism. To the north, they reached the upper reaches of the Sindhu River (the present Indus). To the south, they reached the island of Simhala (the present Sri Lanka).

Central Asian mountains centered on the Pamir Plateau, located in a key point of east-west transportation, were the originals of many rivers (Indus, Amu, Syr Darya, Tarim and etc.) and a meeting place for the ancient world's major civilizations (ancient India, Persia, China, Greece, Rome and etc.) The present Kashmir, Pakistan and Afghanistan in the upper Indus were once affected by ancient Indian civilization, and then influenced by Greece culture after Alexander the Great, the Macedonian king, marched east in the late 4th century B.C. Buddhist stories preached by monks who dispatched by Asoka, deeply touched the residents of north India, inspired the new thinking about Buddha myths and images of the believers in Gandhara (present-day Peshawar,Pakistan), Kubha (Kashmira, present-day Kashimir) etc.

In the middle of the 1st century A.D., two hundred years after the Ta-yueh-chih people from Northwest China to Ta-hsia (The Greek Bactrian empire, today's upper Amu Darya), they became a stronger power, and built Kushan empire, and reached its peak during the reign of the third generation of Kings Kanishka. The capital moved south to Gandhara, and their territories expanded to Indus and Ganges rivers. Kanishka was another king who supported and promoted Buddhism after Asoka. With his support, Buddhist monks held the fourth Buddhist assembly in Kashmir, Kubha therefore became the original place of Mahayana Buddhism. Mahayana is a theology which combines what the Buddha said with various legends and magics of Gandhara, Kubha, Uddiyana and the Greek and Roman interpretations of the images of gods. It goes beyond the original Buddhism along the Ganges river. In order to win people's trust, they created many Buddhist relics in northern India. There were four great towers in central India(Fig.2), as well as in north India; The shadow of Buddha has appeared in the city of Gaya, also in the city of Naga. There was the Usnisa in the Hidda city, lies on the border of Naga, and the Buddha's bowl in Purushapura (according to *Records of Buddhist Kingdoms*, and *Records of the Western Regions of Great Tang*). Meanwhile, Jataka stories such as "The Tathagata's Subjugation of the Evil Dragon""Feeding a Hungry Tiger and Her Cubs with the Prince's Own Body""Offering One's Head to People in Need""Did Own Eyes for eagle""Cut Own Flesh to Feed the Pigeons""The King Shoots Shanzi" etc. and the place where tales happened were made up (according to *Records of Buddhist Kingdoms*, and *Records of Song Yun's Journey*). Emperor Kanishka's desire and action to revitalize Buddhism made Gandhara the second Buddhist Holy Land outside the Ganges valley.

The popularity of Mahayana Buddhism in Gandhara changed the tradition of metaphorizing Buddha with something such as throne, footprints, holy trees, pagodas, stone pillars, lotus, Dharmachakra, elephants, lions and deer from Asoka tome, then painted or sculpted the Buddha as human form for the first time, which announced the Buddhist Image period coming (Figs.3-6). At this time, a large number of stories about Buddha, Maitreya and Jataka stories were carved with a local cyan schist, and marl or plaster. The Buddha's apperance seems reserved, and he has a more favorable Apollo-like face, standing or siting, always wearing soft underwear and robe. Different from Buddha image, Bodhisattva image often wears various of jewelry on her body and Athens-style sandals on her feet. Buddhist art of Gandhara is characterized by Hellenism step into a period of great prosperity. In the Ganges river basin under the rule of the Kushan Dynasty, influenced by Gandhara, the Mathura Art created a large number of exquisite Buddhist statues made of red or yellow sandstone. Buddha images are always shown as monks with a strong body. Bodhisattva images always wear coronet with slight smile on the face. In the Gupta Dynasty of India after the 4th century, the above two types of art were further integrated, with the prominent representation of the Gupta style of Buddha art including thin clothes cling to the body and low eyes.

Xinjiang is the first site for Buddhism to spread eastward. It should have been before the Christine era when Indian monks crossed Pamir and first entered Xinjiang. In the era of Kanishka, the radiant light of Buddha's teachings in northern India first light up the mountains and rivers of Central Asia, and the eastward spread of Buddhism became stronger. From the Hinayana Sutras, The Sutra of 42 Sections, a translation done by monks Kashyapa-matanga and Dharmaranya who came from India to the "White Horse Temple" in Luoyang of China during the reign of Emperor Ming of the Eastern Han Dynasty, to the study of Chan of Hinayana of An Shigao, and the study of Chan of Mahayana of Lokaksema and Zhu Foshuo, proved that the Chinese Buddhism inherit Western theories during the 1st-2nd centuries A.D. indeed. From Zhu Shixing who went on a pilgrimage to the Western Regions for Buddhist scriptures, to the biographies of Kumarajiva and Fa Xian about Countries in the Western Regions, which proved that Xinjiang Buddhism flourished during the 3rd-4th century A.D. Although we don't entirely clear about the footprints of Buddhism in Xinjiang, there is no doubt that Buddhism spread to Xinjiang earlier than to the Han areas. Probably Hinayana was popular all over south of Xinjiang first, then Mahayana flourished. At that time, Hinayana was popular in Qiuci (now Kucha), Yanqi, Shanshan (now Ruoqiang), Qiemo and so on, while Mahayana existed in Khotan (now Hetian), Zihe (now Yecheng), Shale (Shule, now Kashgar) and so on. People built pagodas and temples, constructed grottoes, wore Buddha's bowls on head (in Shale), expounded Buddhism, taken Buddha images in procession, scattered flowers with a solemn atmosphere. The continuous impact of the arrival of Gandhara Buddhist art has promoted the cultural prosperity of each city in Xinjiang. Due to lack of stone materials, Xinjiang Buddhist art composed of clay sculpture, wall painting and wood carvings. The Buddhist booming in Xinjiang became a lighthouse to lead the Buddhism of Han areas to glory.

Chinese Buddhism began in the Eastern Han Dynasty, brewed in Wei and Jin Dynasties, flourished in the Sixteen States Period, boomed in the Southern and Northern Dynasties, matured in Sui and Tang Dynasties, revived in Song, Liao, Jin and Yuan Dynasties, and declined in Ming and Qing Dynasties. Among these historical periods, the Sixteen States Period and the Southern and Northern Dynasties are the key. Buddhism came from the west in two ways: south sea route and northwest land route. In brief, Buddhism took the silk road as the main line. If the road monks taken to spread Buddhism from Ta-yueh-chih and Kushan to east was a way back home, Buddhism blossomed in China after the 4th century in fact benefited from a historic opportunity of the great migration in the Sixteen Kingdoms period.

Although Buddhism was brought to China during the Eastern Han Dynasty, the imperial court only allowed the people of the Western Regions to set up temples in cities, regarded the Buddha as a god of minorities in the west, people of Han nationality were not allowed to leave home and become monks. After Wei and Jin Dynasties, the ban on Buddhism gradually relaxed. At the end of the West Jin Dynasty, the world was in chaos. Minorities from the west and north of China such as Huns, Xianbei, Jie, Di, Qiang and so on set up political power one by one to fight for the throne. Buddhism as the religion of barbarians, had not only been established as the national church by the rulers of minorities which used the reason of "Buddhism supports the regulations of the kingly government, and enriches the good nature of humanity and wisdom" ("Treatise on Buddhism and Taoism" of The Book of Wei, which is no longer indicated in the following quotations), but also has become the spiritual support for the Han and Minorities who suffered from displace or deep distress. The first advocates of Buddhism were Shi Le and Shi Hu, the Jie Emperors of the Later Zhao Dynasty. They worshiped Fotucheng, an eminent monk from the Western Regions, as a great luminary, widely built Buddhist monastery, taught Buddhism to disciples, participated in the national affairs. Shi Hu openly declared: "I was born in the border soil, became the king, and expanded into the Central Plains. Buddha is the god of the western minorities who we should believe in. People of the eastern nations and Zhao, who have given up their obscene sacrifices and willing to believe in Buddhism, could be allowed to become monks." "Therefore, both the minorities who came to the Central Plains and the indigenous people of Jin Dynasty believed in Buddhism" ("Fotucheng from India" of the book *Biographies of Eminent Monks*). Buddhism in Central Plains met the first short climax, and the thought of Buddha could save the world was deeply rooted in people's heart. Then, the Di Emperor Fu Jian of the Former Qin Dynasty and the Qiang Emperor Yao Xing of the Later Qin Dynasty successively worshipped Buddhism, and a large number of master monks appeared successively such as Shi Daoan, Kumarajiva, Buddhabhadra etc. They translated and preached the Buddha's teaching, established precepts and practiced meditation. At that time, Chang'an became the center of Buddhism in China. Around the same time, the Qifu regime in the Western Qin Dynasty and the Juqu regime in the Northern Liang Dynasty also pushed the Buddhism in Longyou and Hexi to its peak. Buddhist belief has become an irreversible trend of the times in Chinese society.

Tuoba Xianbei, the founder of the Northern Wei Dynasty, came from the depths of the Da-Hinggan Mountains, nomadized in north in the late Eastern Han Dynasty, began to expand in Wei and Jin Dynasties. After five Minorities fought for supremacy, Tuoba Xianbei took on the historical mission of cleaning up the remnants of the Central Plains. Tuoba Gui, the Emperor Daowu, established the Northern Wei Dynasty and set Pingcheng as capital in 398. Tuoba Tao, the Emperor Taiwu, unified north China in 439, and then conquered the Western Regions (now Xinjiang) in 448. Tuoba Hong, the Emperor Xiaowen, moved the capital to Luoyang in 494. The Northern Wei Dynasty was divided into the Eastern and Western Wei Dynasties in 534, which were soon replaced by the Northern Qi Dynasty and the Northern Zhou Dynasty respectively. Tuoba Xianbei did not know that there was Buddha before, however their worship of the Buddha was almost crazy from Pingcheng to Luoyang, so Weishou described the matter in the original test "Treatise on Buddhism and Taoism" of his book *The Book of Wei* that "From the time Wei took possession of the Empire until it surrendered it, the Buddhist scriptures that circulated and were collected in the central plains which were in all four hundred and fifteen works, totalling one thousand nine hundred and nine rolls. After Zhengguang the Empire had many anxieties, royal service was most frequent. Thereupon registered subjects, wherever they happened to be, joined one another in entering the clergy. They made a pretense of loving the life of a shramana, but in fact they were evading conscripted service. Such an extreme of hypocrisy, since the Middle Kingdom had acquired the Law of Buddha, there had nerve been. By a rough count the community of monks and nuns was two millions. The temples were more than thirty thousand. The rampant evils, unabated, have come to this, and over them persons of knowledge sigh deeply." Meanwhile, Xiao Yan, the Emperor Liangwu in the south of the Yangtze River, also lost his lives and country because of his superstitious of Buddhism, leaving futurities with sadness such as "Of the four hundred and eighty temples built by the Southern Dynasty, many towers and terraces still remain erect in the misty rain." The prosperity of Chinese Buddhism turned to decline at its peak.

B.
The historical reasons for the creation of Yungang Grottoes

Yungang Grottoes are located at the southern foot of Wuzhou Mountain, 16 kilometers west of Datong City and on the north bank of Wuzhou River (now Shili River), and used to be called Wuzhou Mountain Grotto Temples or Daijing Lingyan Temples in the Northern Wei Dynasty. The grottoes were dug into the mountain about 1 kilometer from east to west. Now there are 254 caves, large or small, including 45 major caves and more than 59,000 statues (Fig.7). The grottoes are grand in scale, the Buddhist statues are abundant in content, the carvings are exquisite in art, and the images are vivid in sense. It can be regarded as the peak of Chinese Buddhist art, and represents the highest level of sculpture in the world in the 5th century.

As for the excavation of the Yungang Grottoes, it is recorded in *Treatise on Buddhism and Taoism* as follows: "Early in Heping (A.D. 460-466) Shixian died and Tanyao replaced him, changed the title name as Comptroller of Shramanas. Earlier, Tanyao, in the year after the restoration of the Law of Buddha, left Zhongshan and proceeded to the capital in obedience to a command. As it happened, the Emperor had come into view on the road, and the royal horse came forward and nibbled at Tanyao's robe. At that time this was thought to mean that even the horse knew a righteous man. The Emperor later honored him with the respect due a teacher. Tanyao humbly begged the Emperor to allow him to dig out the mountain wall of Wuzhou Pass, west of the capital, opened up five caves, and carved Buddha images in them, the tallest to be seventy feet high, the second tallest sixty feet high, with carvings and decorations superb, a crowning glory to the world." The Wuzhou Pass mentioned in this article is located in the north of the western cliff of Yungang Grottoes, and it's a traffic fortress from the Mongolian Plateau to the Han nationality area since the king Wuling of Zhao Dynasty. The main structure of Wuzhou Mountain is sandstone, which is familiar to the Buddhist from the west. The five Buddha grottoes suggested to excavate by Tanyao, namely Caves No.16 to 20 in Yungang today, are called "The Five Tanyao Caves" by scholars. Zhou Yiliang said in the book *Notes on Stone Buddha Images of Yungang* that "The excavation of Grottoes began after Tanyao met the Emperor in the second year of Xingan in Northern Wei Dynasty, or after Tanyao became the Comptroller of Shramanas? We don't know. The point is that the time to start digging was during the eight years from the second year of Xingan (A.D. 453) to the first year of Heping (A.D. 460)".

The excavation of "The Five Tanyao Caves" set off a construction boom of the Wuzhou Mountain Grotto Temples. Starting from the reign of Emperor Wencheng, after Emperor Xianwen and his mother Feng, to Emperor Xiaowen moving the capital, the royal family operated for about 40 years and completed the excavation of all the large caves and statues. Meanwhile, near the Yungang Grottoes, such as the Luyeyuan Grottoes, Qingciyao Grottoes, Lubanyao Grottoes, Wuguantun Grottoes, Jiaoshan temple Grottoes had also been completed one after another. During this period, private funds were widely absorbed. Nobles and ministers, officials from all over the country, men and women disciples had participated in the construction of grottoes in the form of individuals, families and societies, either building a grotto or building a wall, either donating a niche or one's labor, had made the Wuzhou Mountain Grotto Temples a grand sight. After moving the capital, the construction of the Wuzhou Mountain Grottoes lasted for 30 years, until the drum of "the Six Towns Uprising" sounded in the fifth year of Zhengguang (A.D. 524).

The initiation of Yungang Grottoes isn't accidental, but the conclusion of many historical inevitability.

Firstly, the new idea of worshiping emperor as Buddha is the key to lead Buddhism flourish in the Northern Wei Dynasty. Emperor Daowu set Pingcheng as the capital, and "Frist made the Five-Storeyed Stupa and the Mount Gridhrakuta and Mount Sumeru halls with paintings and decorations. In addition, a lecture hall, a meditation hall and cells for shramanas, were built with detailed decorations". About the same time, appointed the eminent monk Faguo who come from the city Zhao (now the Zhao County of Hebei Province) as Daoren Tong, the chief to command monks and Buddhists. "Faguo had always used to say, 'Taizu is enlightened and he loves the Dharma. He is the Tathagata at present. Shramanas must and should pay him all homage.' Then he would always do obeisance. Faguo would say to others, 'He who propagates the teaching of the Buddha is the lord of man. I am not doing obeisance to the Emperor, but merely worshipping the Buddha.'" Before that, Buddhist monks who came to China from the Western Regions piously worshipped their Buddha and did not need to worship emperor. However, after the Sixteen Kingdoms of the Eastern Jin Dynasty, the Han nationality monks became mainstream, who once were the subjects of the emperor, now became disciples of Shakyamuni. Therefore, whether shramanas need to worship the emperor, that is whether to recognize and accept the management of the kingdom, has become a question that must be answered by the northern and southern Buddhists. In this regard, the master Hui Yuan, who lived in seclusion in Lushan, wrote a treatise "Controversy over Shramana's Salutation to the Emperor" which represented the position of the southern monks, and the words and deeds of Faguo showed the attitude of the northern monks. As the disciples of Fotucheng, they chose the opposite ways, and the development of Buddhism in North and South was obviously different. Although what Faguo said tends to be flattery and sophistry, it absorbed the successful experience of Fotucheng in promoting Buddhadharma relied on the power of the country and influencing the politics with methods and tactics; it followed the famous saying of Shi Daoan, "If you don't follow the ruler of the state, it's difficult to establish the position of the Dharma." Perhaps Buddhism can't develop without the support of the emperor, who also needs to be deified. By integrating emperor with Buddha, Faguo put forward the new theory that emperor is the living Buddha, skillfully turned the disciples of Shakyamuni back to the followers of the emperor, which catered to the psychological needs of the supreme ruler and transcended the religious behavior into the will of the state, which laid the foundation for the prosperity of Buddhism in the Northern Dynasty. Later, Shixian, the director of monks in the Northern Wei Dynasty, made a sacred statue for Emperor Wencheng, ordered that it must look like the Emperor. Tanyao dug grottoes and carved statues for five imperial ancestors in Wuzhou Mountain, in fact, this is the recreation and implementation of the theory of Faguo. Therefore, the Wuzhou Mountain Grottoes was included in the royal project, which became the voluntary action for several generations of emperors to build family temples.

Secondly, the formation of the Buddhist Center in Pingcheng made it possible to build large-scale Buddhist images. From the period when Emperor Daowu founded the Country to the time when Emperor Taiwu ended the situation where warlords had occupied different regions, the plundering and emigrating policy promoted by the Northern Wei Dynasty that helped Pingcheng, the once remote county, quickly became the political, military, economic and cultural center of China. Pingcheng had later become the new peak of oriental international metropolis due to the conquest of the Western Regions. When noble bureaucrats, Confusion scholars, Taoists, Buddhists, skilled craftsmen, renters and businessmen as well as all kinds wealth like gold and silver gathered in Pingcheng, people's belief in Buddhism was also heating up at the same time. Especially in the fifth year of Taiyan of the Northern Wei Dynasty (A.D. 439), "Treatise on Buddhism and Taoism" said that "Liangzhou people from Zhang Gui onward for generations believed in Buddhism. Dunhuang was close to the Western Regions, and the clergy and laity both acquired the old fashions. The villages, one after the other, had many reliquaries and temples. During Tai-yan period, Liangzhou was pacified and the people of the country moved to the capital. The shramanas and Buddhist practices both went east, and both the images and the doctrine increasingly prospered". The Hexi Corridor under the jurisdiction of Liangzhou (also called Guzang, now Wuwei, Gansu province) has been a place where Chinese and Western cultures have integrated since ancient times, and it was also the first stop site for monks from the Western Regions to enter Middle-earth places. At the beginning of the 4th century, Zhang Gui served as the Cishi (provincial governor) in Liangzhou, where the worship of Buddha has been popular among people. In 417, Liu Yu, the great general of the Eastern Jin Dynasty attacked and destroyed the Yao's regime (the Later Qin), monks in Chang'an city scattered away, which had made the Buddhism in Hexi the most outstanding one in China. Emperor Taiwu migrated 30,000 officials and civilians in Liangzhou (including 3,000 monks who were captured while guarding the city) to the capital city. This looked like that the Buddhism in Hexi had been completely "relocated", making Pingcheng the new center of Chinese Buddhism. The skilled monks from Liangzhou who once witnessed the Buddhist events in Hindu as well as the Western Regions and took part in the excavation and meditation of the Hexi and Longyou grottoes such as Dunhuang Mogao Grottoes, Wuwei Tiantishan Grottoes, Yongjing Bingling Temple Grottoes and Tianshui Maijishan Grottoes, had become the major forces of building the future Buddhist temples and grottoes in Pingcheng.

Thirdly, Emperor Taiwu's order of destroying Buddhism stimulated the rapid development of Buddhism in the Northern Wei Dynasty in an opposite way. The eastward migration of Liangzhou monks also triggered the first struggle between Buddhism and Taoism in the history of China while promoting the rapid prosperity of Buddhism in Pingcheng. Under the influence of the Songshan Taoist Kou Qianzhi and Situ Cui Hao, Emperor Taiwu decreed to destroy Buddhism in the seventh year of Taiping-Zhenjun (A.D. 446). In a short time, in the folk of the Northern Wei Dynasty, "Of the gold, silver, treasure and images, as well as the scriptures and treatises, much be concealed. But buildings and reliquaries wherever the proclamation reached were destroyed." However, the stronger the destruction of Buddhism was, the demand for it was more intense. In the first year of Xingan (A.D. 452), not long after Tuoba Jun became Emperor Wencheng, decreed to recover Buddhism under the request of ministers. "The emperor ordered the Buddhist statues to be built. The Buddhist were afraid of it being ruined again, claimed that the materials of wood sometimes decayed, the soil sometimes collapsed and the gold sometimes shone. Only by covering the Buddhist Statues with stone room, can ensure those statues stay safe. However, the statues also had risks of being excavating and stealing if they were built too small. If the height one foot is not enough, make a few feet. If a few feet are not enough, do our best to get a few ten-feet. Only add up to hundreds or even thousands of feet, can make it last forever and never break, and make people who see it feel awe." (*Notes of Yungang Grottoes*, by Zhu Yizun). Therefore, "The Five Tanyao Buddhist Statues" came out at this historic moment.

Fourthly, recalling Shakyamuni's past in Mrigadava, to build the holy place of the oriental Buddhism. Mrigadava, the Deer Garden, was the place where Shakyamuni gave his first discourse after his awakening, now in the suburbs of current Benares, India. The Deer Garden in the Northern Wei Dynasty was in the north of Pingcheng Palace. Emperor Daowu built the garden wall in the second year of Tianxing (A.D. 399). "The covering area was vast that reached Baideng Mountain to the east and West Mountain to the west" ("The Biography of Gaoche" of *The Book of Wei*). The west mountain of the Deer Garden was once closed and forbidden for cutting firewood by Emperor Daowu, Tuoba Gui. Altars were built for sacrifice in Wuzhou Mountain where was regarded as a holy place, during Emperor Ming-yuan, Tuoba Si, ruled the country. After Emperor Taiwu pacified Liangzhou, the mountain gradually became the place where the western monks quarried stone, carved Buddhist statues, excavated grottoes and practiced meditation. Therefore, the Deer Garden in Pingcheng and in India naturally paired and resonated in the minds of Liangzhou monks. In particular, the emergence of "The Five Tanyao Buddhist Statues" greatly inspired the young Emperor Xianwen, Tuoba Hong, and strengthened his confidence in imitating the shrine site of Western Heavens and establishing the oriental Deer Garden. As described in *Deer Garden Fu* by Gao Yun, "The Emperor that succeeded the throne was born smart and visionary. Recalling the past of the Deer Garden, thriving the doctrine which had three turns of the wheel when the Buddha preached in the Deer Park. To develop the profound doctrine forever, then always have something to place emotion after thousands of years. Therefore, decreed master to select craftsmen even from the Western Regions. By careful observation and reflection, imitating Buddha statues. Statues were vivid like real person and glittering with gold put onto. Temples built against the cliff were extremely high. Beams were designed on the floating pillars, and beautiful lotus were carved on caisson ceilings. Decorated withpatterns in various forms, filled it with noble stories. It just looked like another Jetavana, but had a different way to become enlightened. The grottoes that the techniques used to build it were superb, the magnificent of it was no one before!" The building of the Wuzhou Mountain Grotto Temples was fully conducted at that time.

Fifthly, the western culture melting into China cocreated the splendid Chinese Buddhist culture. The Northern Wei Dynasty's conquest of the Western Regions directly ushered in the second climax of the East-West cultural exchange in Chinese history. As a metropolis at the eastern end of the Silk Road, Pingcheng quickly became a place where foreign monks and merchants gathered. The popularity of building grottoes and carving Buddhist statues in India was introduced into China through Xinjiang, Hexi, Guanlong and Pingcheng. And in Pingcheng, Buddhism reached its climax. The creation of the Wuzhou Mountain Grottoes was firstly conducted by Liangzhou monks and craftsmen who brought the Western-style Buddhist statue art (Fig.8-9). Later, the creation helped by foreign monks who came from ancient India, Simhala and other western countries, and carried Buddhist scriptures, statues and illustrated books to come to China with trade caravan and missions. After that,Tanyao proposed to collect precious Buddhist statues all over the country to the capital city. Finally, Xuzhou monks and craftsmen went north to preside over the Yungang Buddhist events, that was also of great importance to the creation of the Wuzhou Mountain Grottoes. The unique and splendid Buddhist paradise in Yungang Grottoes was designed and created by the extraordinary joint efforts of generations of monks and masters as well as craftsmen.

As the earliest appeared large-scale grottoes in the east of Xinjiang, while shocking the world, the magnificence and brilliance of the Wuzhou Mountain Grotto Temples became a model for leading and promoting the construction climax of Buddhist grottoes in the Northern Dynasty. From Yungang to the east are the Wanfotang Grottoes in Yixian, Liaoning Province. To the south are the Longmen Grottoes in Luoyang and Gongxian Grottoes in Henan Province, Tianlongshan Grottoes in Taiyuan, Shanxi Province, Xiangtangshan Grottoes in Handan, Hebei Province. To the west are some grottoes in Gansu province, such as the Southern Grottoes in Jingchuan, Northern Grottoes in Qingyang, Maijishan Grottoes in Tianshui, Bingling temple Grottoes in Yongjing, Mogao Grottoes in Dunhuang and so on. All these grottoes have been influenced by the Wuzhou Mountain Grottoes. During the nearly 200 years from Tanyao excavated grottoes in the Northern Wei Dynasty to the time when Buddhist monks Daoxuan saluted in the distance in the early Tang Dynasty, the Lingyan Temple (the Wuzhou Mountain Grottoes) in Daijing (Pingcheng) had always been the holy place for Chinese monks no matter how the political situation changed. The excavation of Yungang Grottoes had a profound impact on the promotion of Grotto Temples and the development of carving art in China.

C.
The masterpiece of eastern Buddhist art

Regarding the art origin of Yungang Grottoes, scholars at home and abroad have discussed abundantly for more than 100 years, such as Egyptian, Greek or Tuoba influence theory, and theories of Gandhara art, Mathura art, Gupta art or West Regions (Xinjiang) art input and etc. Among them, Gandhara art, Mathura element as well as Xinjiang style were the most popular. Emperor Wencheng of the Northern Wei Dynasty

"Early in Tai-an there were five barbarian monks from Lion Land, Ye-she-yi-duo, Buddhanandi and others, who beared three Buddha images, arrived in the capital. They all said that they had traversed all the countries of the Western Regions and seen the Buddha's image and top-knot. The kings of the foreign lands, one after the other, had all sent artisants to copy the form, but there had been none who could equal that made by Buddhanandi. If one stood ten-odd paces away from it and looked, it was bright, but the closer one came to it the dimmer it became. Also, a barbarian monk from Kashgar went to the capital and presented the Buddha's Patra and portrait." The above records show that the Buddhist statues in Pingcheng and Yungang have a certain inheritance relationship with Indian and Xinjiang art. However, we will always be ambiguous when studying and observing the Buddhist statues in Gandhara and Mathura, because there are few things exactly the same as the Yungang Grottes. Those differences in style, artistic conception as well as fashion clearly indicate a breakage in the cultural and artistic relationship between each other, or in other words, a vacancy exists in it. On the contrary, we will feel much more familiar and genial when observing the early Buddhist remains in Xinjiang. The feelings are generated from Kucha Kizil Grottoes, Pagoda with centersquare style from Xinjiang Buddhist remains, and in particular, the yellow-clay sculptures that are convenient to facsimile, their various types full-moon-shaped faces and exotic appearances which produced in the north and south of the Tarim Basin (Fig.10).

Based on the historical background analysis of Buddhism's eastward spreading, what monks and craftsmen who came from Liangzhou originally brought to Pingcheng could only be the Liangzhou style or the Western Region style, and the Liangzhou style is actually a mixed art of the North and South Buddhism in West Regions. It should be regarded as a historical inevitability that the Xinjiang style Gandhara art and even Mathura art are transferred and reproduced in Yungang Grottoes. Especially to the Buddhist Image in places like Yuzhou and Zihe where Mahayana Buddhism prevails. Analyzed from the Yungang Grottoes projection itself, Liangzhou monks and craftsmen were the major people for planning and designing. The aesthetic wishes of the Xianbei and the Han Nationality have naturally permeated in the Buddhist statues, paintings as well as statuary rules that these monks and craftsmen have based on, no matter that was directly or indirectly imitating the Western Regions, its blueprints were approved by the Emperor in the Northern Wei Dynastyor other related government officials. Craftsmen who excavated grottoes included some monks from Liangzhou, but most of them were Han people from all over the Central Plain, which has resulted in the massive using of traditional Chinese carving techniques and expressing methods. We believe that the Westernstyle design and Chinese-style craftsmanship are the biggest characteristics of Yungang Grottoes. Of course, the later, the heavier weight of Chinese tradition, the stronger consciousness of independent innovation. This is why the Yungang sculpture art is not simply similar to India, Central Asia and Xinjiang (Fig.11-12).

As the first wonderful fruit that Western Buddhism has bred in the Chinese land, Yungang Grottoes changed the artistic mode of the grotto temples in the east of the Pamirs, which were mainly composed of clay sculptures, murals and wood carvings. Directly according to the largescale grotto architecture in India, Yungang Grottoes firstly created a majestic, all-stone-carved Buddhist grottoes in China. At the same time, by widely absorbing the essence of Chinese and foreign sculpture art, being inclusive and integrated, Yungang Grottoes became a treasure house of early Chinese Buddhist art. The excavation of Yungang Grottoes is roughly divided into three periods, namely three phases. The early phase: the carving of "The Five Tanyao Caves" at the time of Emperor Wencheng; The middle phase: the large grottoes and statues built by the royal family of Emperor Xianwen, Empress Dowager Feng and Emperor Xiaowen; The later phase: caves and niches made up by folk people since the capital has been moved to Luoyang city. The sculpture of Yungang Grottoes are divided into two categories: the western style and the newdesign Chinese style. It shows the gradual Sinicization and secularization of the Western Buddhism in a concentrated way, which can be regarded as a milestone in the development of Chinese Buddhist art.

"The Five Tanyao Caves" are typical representatives of Yungang Grottoes and also the top-level works of sculpture art that spread to China from the West Regions. The cassock worn by the giant Buddha statues causes his body to be covered up or partially exposed, that looks very heavy and likes wool textiles, which is undoubtedly the typical clothing features in the pastoral countries of Central Asia. The Buddha statues are designed with tall Uchnicha, broad forehead and chubby cheeks, high nose bridge and deep-set eyes, long and slender eyebrows and eyes, upward mouth corners, shoulder-length ears, tall and straight robust body, which can make people feel that the expression is solemn but amiable, the vigour is grand and magnificent. As the great Buddhist monk of Tang Dynasty Daoxuan said, "The Buddha statues in the Song and Qi Dynasties look like men with ambition and action, with thick lips, high nose bridge, long eyes and full cheeks." (*Buddhism Digest*, volume II, Song Dynasty). In particular, the great open-air Buddha statue in the No.20 cave (Fig.13) is majestic, magnificent and full of vitality, which fully and vividly expresses the Tuoba Xianbei's national spirit of fierceness and strength, ruggedness and boldness, generosity and intelligence, giving people a soul shock. However, ten disciples that on the east and west sides of the major Buddha in the No. 18 cave, are Western races and different in appearances and expressions, showing the obvious characteristics of the Western Regions.

After finishing succession to the throne (A.D. 446), Emperor Xianwen redeployed the Wuzhou Moumtain Grottoes Project, and accelerated the pace of construction expansion, diversification of grotto shapes as well as pluralism of image content. Till the eighteenth year of Tai-he under Emperor Xiaowen's rule (A.D. 494), the capital was moved to Luoyang, the building of Yungang Grottoes reached its peak. Grottoes excavated during this period include 4 groups of double-grottoes, No.7 and No.8 caves, No.9 and No.10 caves, No.1 and No.2 caves, as well as No.5 and No.6 caves, and one group of triple grottoes, No.11, No.12 and No.13 caves (Figure 14), and also the unfinished No.3 cave. Regarding the shape of the grottoes, there are not only dome-shaped, but also square-shaped which had tower-column in the middle as well as grottoes with front and back halls. In the shape of Buddhist niches, there are house-shaped niche, curtainshaped niche and compound-type niche added to the original round-arch niche, lintel-shaped niche and cap-shaped niche. Compared with the early dome-shaped grottoes, the vast emergence of grottoes with square plan significantly increased the carving areas, and the carving content and form became more complicated. The top of the Grotto is mostly carved with caisson ceiling, while the walls are carved with the design way of up and down, left and right segments. Although the subject of Buddhist statues in this period was still mainly Shakyamuni and Maitreya, the content of the sculptures has continued to increase and the number of Buddhist scriptures relied on also increased significantly. The commonly popular Buddhist images in shrines were Shakyamuni in teaching or meditation, Shakyamuni and Prabhutaratna sitting side by side teaching together, the seven Buddhas, Vimalakirti and Manjushri discuss Buddhism, and the cross-legged Bodhisattva in Bodhisattva or Buddha costume. The images of protectors of the Buddha-truth are beginning to carve on both sides of the door arch. The story in niches and continuous carving about the Buddha Shakyamuni's life and previous lives are placed on the most intuitive position on the wall. The images of patron who offer money or materials were carved below niches or the wall with a symmetrical arrangement. Architectural shapes such as stupas, pillars and hip roofs vividly appeared. The images of Buddhist statues were in diverse kinds, such as apsaras, bhikshu, vira, vajra, Deva-musician and Devadancer, Deva-donor, variety animal and flower patterns, and so on. So far, this Yungang Grottoe art treasure-house basically formed.

No.7 and No.8 caves are the earliest double-caves in Yungang Grottoes, the flat ceiling are decorated with lotus and apsaras patterns, giving the traditional Chinese architectural style the romance of Buddhist fairyland. The three-headed and four-armed statues on both sides of the arch of No.7 cave wear pointed hat, showing great characteristics of Central Asia and Western Asia. The statues on both sides of the arch of No. 8 cave are the Maheshvara with three heads and eight arms who are riding a bull, and the Kumarakadeva with five heads and six arms who are riding a bird. Those images are derived from Shiva and Vishnu in ancient Indian mythology, one can destroy the universe while another can create the world. This phenomenon of transforming great gods of Brahmanism into protective divinities of Buddhism is a reflection of Indian Tantra, which totally from Western Buddhism images and is the out-of-print remains of the Chinese and Western Grotto Temples. No.9 and No.10 caves are traditional Chinese palace-style buildings, but the front courtyard of the grotto is composed of pillars that carried by lions and elephants and architectural shapes, which are mixed with ancient Indian, Greek and Roman architectural styles. The Vajra with feather style crown on the head on both sides of the arch in the rear chamber is mighty and brave, which is typical in the protective divinities images in Yungang double-grottoes. No.5 and No.6 caves are very grand in scale. The former is a great Buddha grotto, the major statue of Buddha in it reaching 17.4 meters high, ranking the highest among Yungang Buddha statues; the latter is a central stupa grotto that is completely designed and complicatedly carved, which is particularly famous in the world for the series of relief continuous carving that describes the life story of Shakyamuni. No.12 cave is also a corridor-style palace grotto, commonly known as "Music cave". On the top place of the north wall of the front room, Deva-musicians hold various Eastern and Western musical instruments, just like a "symphony orchestra", which is a precious material for studying the history of ancient Chinese music. Those magnificent grotto buildings, colorful stone carvings and great creations that shock the world are immortal masterpieces that Chinese nation has dedicated to all mankind.

The mid-term construction of Yungang Grottoes was influenced by the Maitreya belief and the Western Pure Land ideology in the Northern Wei Dynasty. While striving to create a "Tushita heaven palace" in the human world, it was in a vigorous development stage based on the past achievements. On the one hand, the Western style and Western charm were still strong and in a dominating place with the continuous influence of the Western image art. On the other hand, Chinesestyle architecture, costumes, carving techniques and aesthetic appeal were gradually revealed with the rising of traditional Chinese power. We can feel that the carvings of statues of Buddha and Bodhisattva mainly imitate Xinjiang clay sculptures. Those various hanging lowtemperature yellow-clay molded sculptures have already been massive produced around Pingcheng city at that time, and are used to decorate pagodas and temples, providing lots of fresh samples for the carving of Yungang Grottoes. Compared with the early sculptures, the midterm construction of statues are still robust and beautiful, but gradually losses their inner fortitude and personality, the carving of which has been stylized like making facsimile reproduction of clay-sculptures. The carving of great Buddhist statues, major Buddha statues as well as some important Buddhist statues is delicate and exquisite, and the carving of ordinary statues are slightly rough. The concise and delicate carving methods of craftsmen seem to appear inadvertently, bringing people a free, lively and untrammelled feeling. Some Buddhist statues started to be built comeliness with moderate face, not fat or thin. The appearance of Buddhist cassock is not limited to rightshoulder-unbuttoned and full-shoulder-covering style, but also includes the style of loose gown with wide girdle. The clothing of the Bodhisattva has also changed. In addition to the precious crown worn on the head, the flower and vine crown being popular, the wearing of necklace of precious stones or other strung together, and clothing that can cover the axilla, has changed to the wearing of ribbons that wrap around arms then drop naturally; the skirts stick to legs which changed to the hem of the skirts flutters out. The tendency that the style of these Buddha's and Bodhisattva's costumes is transformed into Hanstyle is clearly a reflection of Emperor Xiaowen's reform in costumes and implement other Han culture policy since the tenth year of Tai-he (A.D. 486). Consequently, it fills the gap in the evolution of Chinese Buddhist art from the "western style and appearance" to "Chinese style and appearance" in the Southern and Northern Dynasties.

In the Yungang Grottoes, we can't tell exactly how long it has taken for Han Nationality to awake its national consciousness. However, because the leadership of monks who from Liangzhou that were deeply influenced by western Buddhism and Buddhist art, it has started to shake since the fifth year of Tai-he (A.D. 481) probably. Subsequently, the great monk in Xuzhou who studies prajna accepted the invitation of Emperor Xiaowen and went north leading his disciples. "Chanting and preaching Buddhism in royal temples in the northwest of Pingcheng, while being the monks' teacher in the capital" ("The Decree of Emperor Xiaowen in the Northern Wei Dynasty of Donating Silks and Vegetarian Diet for the Great monk Huiji's Death" of the book *An Enlarged Collection of the Expositions of Truth*), the Buddhism atmosphere in the capital Pingcheng has hence changed. In the thirteenth year of Tai-he (A.D. 489), the style of statues with loose gown and wide girdle, and elegant and thin image that were set in the niche on the outer wall of Yungang No. 11 cave, which has become fashionable ever since. If the earliest Buddha statues with loose gown and wide girdle in Yungang No. 6 cave is still in the "western style and appearance", many sculptures of niches on the outer walls of No. 11, No. 12 and No. 13 caves are completely changed to Chinese style from the western style.

After Emperor Xiaowen moving the capital to Luoyang, Pingcheng was still the northern capital of the Northern Wei Empire. Although the royal projects in Yungang was basically finished, the popular trend in folk to excavate caves and carve statues was still strong. Although there are fewer large caves, small and medium caves and niches spread all over the cliff face from east to west. These late grottoes with large quantities are complex in types and various in style, while the interior of these caves is becoming more and more square. The central pagoda caves, caves with four-walls and three-niches as well as multiple-niches in main wall were the popular type among that period. The subject and content of the statue tend to be modeled and simplified. All the Buddha statues were having a loose gown with wide girdle, thin face, slender neck and shoulders as well as ethereal and void expressions. All the Bodhisattva statues were designed tall and slender with crossed ribbons and exclusive expressions. These statues give people a beautiful, handsome, extraordinary as well as refined feeling, which obviously is consistent with the Chinese people's understanding of the image of gods. The folds on the lower part of the Buddhist statue's clothing are more and more overlapping, the lintel of niches and the tent-shaped emblazonries are becoming more and more complicated, and so are the carvings on the cliffs outside the grottoes. The above-mentioned styles and characteristics are nearly the same as the Buddhist statues in Longmen Grottoes in the Northern Wei Dynasty, marking Chinese people's introduction of western Buddhism and Buddhist art and the initial end of its absorption process.

D.
The great contribution of Pingcheng era to Chinese Buddhism

The 97 years since the Northern Wei Dynasty has settled its capital in Pingcheng were the critical period for the growth and prosperity of Chinese Buddhism. In addition to the impacts on the construction of later grottoes and the development of art brought by Yungang Grottoes, the Buddhist theories, the monk official systems, the systems for monks and nuns as well as the pattern of monastery economy introduced, shaped, established and strengthened in this period have also made a profound impact on the development of later Buddhism.

a) The establishment of the idea of Buddhism serving the ruler

The book *History of Buddhism in Han, Wei, Western Jin and Eastern Jin, Southern and Northern Dynasties* written by Tang Yongtong describes: "When Shakyamuni was still alive in the ordinary world, Prasenajit had shown great respect to the Buddha, Buddhism and Sangha, many Buddhist scriptures were appreciated as wonderful conversations. Afterwards both Emperor Asoka of the Maurya Dynasty and Kanishka of the Kushana Dynasty believed in Buddhism extremely and carried Buddhism forward, the disciples of Shakyamuni joined them in pushing Buddhism to its climax." Therefore, it can be deduced that Buddhism has been keenly connected with politics for a long time. *The Handing Down of Buddha's Teachings* has recorded the talking when Kanadeva was preaching Buddhism in the Southern Hindu: "The branches of the tree will be hard to grow if it is not gotten pruning; and Buddhism will be difficult to preach if the ruler of the people doesn't believe it." This kind of thinking that relies on the king to promote Buddhism, which is far earlier than Shi Daoan's perception that "Buddhism will be difficult to develop if it doesn't depend on the king of the country", should belong to the Buddhist tradition. However, since Buddhism was introduced to China, clear official restrictions on this religion had been made since the Han and Wei Dynasties. People of Han Nationality were not allowed to be monks, and the government couldn't worship the deva of foreign nationalities. Therefore, those foreign Buddhists came together with businessmen could only slowly promote Buddhism in the folk with the manner of treating people with medicine or witchcraft, telling fortunes as well as worshiping the God for praying for rain. Buddhism could only hide its great wisdom of helping the country and do good things, and preach by relying on the Huang-Lao Philosophy and metaphysics. Such imperceptible promoting manners, which was similar to divination, had lasted for over 3 centuries until Shi Family in the Later Zhao Dynasty took the lead in worshipping the Buddha. Fotucheng was the first man that promoted the integration between Buddhism and the regime in the Central Plain. *Biographies of Eminent Monks* recorded: "There are often hundreds of people following the monks who are preaching Buddhism. The total Buddhists before or after them even have reached nearly ten thousand. These followers have built 893 Buddhist temples in places where they have traveled. The propagation of Buddhism has reached its prosperity like never before." Although the Later Zhao was a short-lived Dynasty, the worship of Buddhism in China had become popular ever since. Faguo in the Northern Wei Dynasty joined the Buddhist about 30 years later after Fotucheng's death. Although it was still unknown that which teacher Faguo followed, but what he had learned were nothing more than Fotudeng's theory of Buddhism. Faguo's theory about promoting Buddhism that worship the King as the current Buddha inherited Fotucheng's experience, which was consistent with Shi Daoan's famous saying and clarified the policy of Buddhism serving the imperator. Therefore, the later Emperor Wencheng fully affirmed Buddha's merits in his edict of recovering Buddhism: "He supports the prohibitions and regulations of kingly government, and enriches the good nature of humanity and wisdom. He drives away many evils and sets forth right perception." Buddhism was thus incorporated into feudal politics and became one of the ruling methods that Chinese Dynasties had always acted on. The thinking that the king was the current Buddha was inherited by the later emperors who believed in Buddhism. Empress Wu Zetian claimed that she was the reincarnation of Maitreya, and built many large statues to reflect it; Emperor Wuzhong of the Ming Dynasty claimed that he was the Daqing

Dharmaraja and the Xitian Yuanming Zizai Dadinghui Buddha (The Buddha who has complete enlightenment, great insight and great wisdom). Both of which inherited the same ruling methods.

b) The formation of monk official system and the publication and enforcement of *Regulations on Monks*

Emperor Daowu in the Northern Wei Dynasty appointed Faguo as "Daoren Tong (the director of Buddhists) who is responsible for the management of monks and Buddhists". It is the earliest record about setting Buddhist official positions in official history books, which marks that Chinese Buddhism has stepped up to the superstructure from the low ebb. Emperor Wencheng renamed Daoren Tong as Shamen Tong (the director of Buddhist monks) in the first year of Heping (460). Because there were so many monks in the capital at that time, Duweina (Wei-na, karmadana) was set as the deputy leader to assist the Shamen Tong. Besides, Jian-fu-cao was set in the government to manage the Buddhist affairs of the whole country. Seng Tong (the director of monks) and Wei-na were set in cities and counties to administrate the local Buddhist monks and nuns. Temples imitated the manage mode of the Western Regions, and set three leading offices: Wei-na, Shang-zuo (Arya) and Si-zhu (Viharasvamin). In the period when Emperor Xiaowen was governing, impacted by the rebellion of Faxiu in the fifth year of Tai-he, on the one hand, the registered residence system for Buddhist monks were strengthened to limit their travelling; on the other hand, Jian-fucao was reorganized as Zhao-xuan and particular officials were prepared to manage monastic affairs. Especially the law, *Regulations on Monks*, which contained 47 items was issued by the Emperor in the seventeenth year of Tai-he, which declared the birth of Chinese monastic systems in a legislative manner. This is the first statute code about monks and nuns promulgated by the country we have known so far, which is different from Asoka's Edicts carved on a stone pillar in the ancient India, and different from commandments self-stipulated by the monks in Hindu since the time of Shakyamuni (there are five sorts of commandments that have been spread to China). This means that monks and nuns as a special social group have been officially recognized by the country. Besides, it also means that such recognition is conditional and must obey national laws. "Upon the emperor whose dynastic title is Shizong accession, in the autumn of the first year of Yongping, an Imperial edict said: Monks are different from secular people, so the laws that apply to them are also different... Since today, all the monks who was guilty of murder or worse shall be punished consistent with secular customs. Other remaining criminals shall be handed over to Zhao-xuan and treated with internal regulations and Regulations on Monks." Monks and nuns in the Northern Wei Dynasty should abide by the national laws externally while obeying the precepts and monk's regulations internally at the same time, so we can see that they enjoyed certain independent rights. Although we don't fully clear for the institution mode of monk officials and monks in Pingcheng in the Northern Wei Dynasty, there is no doubt that it's the origin of the Sui and Tang Dynasties system.

c) The birth of temple economy and its independent development

The earliest lifestyle for Buddhist monks in India was mainly to beg for food along the streets or be given food by believers. Probably due to the gradual increasing impacts of Buddhism in the later years, Buddhist temples gradually had its own dependent people and fixed economic income. Emperor Taiwu in the Northern Wei Dynasty conquered Liangzhou, a great number of monks were arrested and moved to the capital, making them go through a tough and poor time. When Emperor Wencheng ordered to recover Buddhism, many temples were actively built in the capital and other places to help monks. Particularly the excavation of the Wuzhou Mountain Grottoes and other grottoes had accumulated a large number of monks and craftsmen. Therefore, how to arrange the food of monks and the labor using naturally became a question that Tanyao, Shamen Tong (the leader of Buddhist), must take the long view to consider. Whereupon "Tanyao reported to the Emperor: 'Ping-qi Hu[1] and other people, who could provide 60 Hu[2] of millet to Seng-cao[3] every year, should be classified as 'Seng-qi Hu'; the millet provided will be classified as 'Seng-qi Su'. In poor harvest year, these millet will be donated to famine refugee. People who commited felony crimes and the official slaves should be classified as "Fo-tu Hu" responsible for cleaning temples, farming and handing in grains every year'. Emperor Gaozong[4] approved Tanyao's suggestions. Consequently, Seng-qi Hu, Seng-qi Su and Fo-tu Hu were all over the cities and counties". Notes: Seng-qi means lots of monks and nuns; Seng-qi Hu means the residents dependent to the mass monks; Seng-qi Su means the grains provided to the mass monks; Fo-tu Hu, also called Si Hu, refers to the slaves that provide services to monks of temples, similar to the lay workers in the Buddhist temple in the Western Region. The emergence of Fo-tu Hu, Seng-qi Hu and Seng-qi Su, satisfied the needs of Buddhist affairs in the Northern Wei Dynasty. That is the symbol of the formation and independence of Chinese temple economy. There were still two kinds of inferior people, Buqu and Nubi in Buddhist temples and Taoist temples till the Tang Dynasty, which were different in the name but same in the meaning with the Northern Wei Dynasty. This emerging temple economy since has become a special form of Chinese landlord manor economy by relying on the extra authority in the politic and economic field, which has always been keenly consistent with feudal society.

d) The formation and inheritance of the political core of Buddhist Sangha

During the Wei and Jin Dynasties, especially the Northern and Southern Dynasties, Chinese Buddhism reached gradually maturity. Both the study of the three divisions of Tripitaka, Sutras, Vinaya and Abhidharma, and the political and economic status of monks and nuns were in a rising period. The Northern areas emphasized more on Dhyana, while the Southern areas emphasized more on the Sutra chanting. Although there were differences in the methods of preaching Buddhism, these areas were the same in terms of classifying religious groups, expanding powers, and seeking fame and fortune. In the middle Tai-he years of the Northern Wei Dynasties, Liangzhou monks who practiced Buddhist meditation and Xuzhou monks who pursued Sutra chanting accumulated together in Pingcheng, which could be described as the first large-scale bout between the North and South Buddhist forces. Although the details are unknown now, it can be completely deduced that the latecomers of Xuzhou monks have occupied the popularity, caused pressure on the Liangzhou old monks, and made them feel lost. Academic differences and political disputes are the causes of the serious confrontations between the two sides. Contradictions and conflicts are inevitable. This struggle started in Pingcheng and was divided into Liangzhou faction and Xuzhou faction. After the capital was moved to Luoyang, the distinction between monks by Dhyana and chanting were continued until the Sui and Tang Dynasties. The second volume of *Record of Luoyang Qielan (Temples)* recorded such a story: in the first year of Xiao-chang (A.D. 525), the monk Huining of Chongzhen Monastery is alive again after death. He told that he had seen that Yama sentenced monks who practiced Buddhist meditation to the heaven and monks who pursued sutra chanting to the Hell. Empress Dowager Ling heard about the story and "immediately invite a hundred Dhyana Monks and often provide for them in the palace... After that, monks in the capital all changed to practice Dhyana meditation and no longer chant Sutra". Notes: the talk of Hui Ning was made up by Dhyana Monks in order to attack Chanting Monks who were advantaged in politics. This is undoubtedly the continuation of the confrontation of Liangzhou monks and Xuzhou monks in the period of Emperor Xiaowen. In principle, from the Northern Wei Dynasty to the Sui and Tang Dynasties, although the regime changed repeatedly, the main force of the ruler had always been the descendants of the northern of Daizhou and the Central Plains. Despite the ebb and flow between these two sides of Buddhist monks, the superior and traditional Buddhist were still from the Liangzhou and Xuzhou Buddhism system.

e) Buddhist Sutra translation in Wuzhou Mountain Grottoes and *The Handing Down of Buddha's Teachings*

The story of Buddhist Sutras entering China reached its first climax in the Sixteen Kingdoms and Southern and Northern Dynasties. Belief in Buddha, Buddhism and Sangha were prosperous in cities like Changan, Liangzhou, Jiankang, Pingcheng and Luoyang. The translation of Buddhist Sutras continued endlessly. "Treatise on Buddhism and Taoism" recorded: "Tanyao, together with Hindu Buddhist Chang-na-xie-she translated 14 new Buddhist sutras." According to the book *Catalogue of Buddhist Scriptures Published in Successive Dynasties* written by Fei Changfang in the Sui Dynasty and other books, the Buddhist leader Tanyao organized many monks to translate Buddhist sutras from the third year of Heping of Emperor Wencheng (A.D. 462) to the tenth year of Tai-he of Emperor Xiaowen (A.D. 486). Their translation works include *The Samadhi Sutra about keep Heart Pure to Obtain Salvation*, *The Handing Down of Buddha's Teachings*, *The Sutra about Buddha Taught to Trapusha and Bhallika*, *Miscellaneous Treasures Sutra*, *Bodhisattvas of Dashabhumi Mahavaipulya Sutra*, *Upaya Heart Treatise*, *The Sutra of Dharani of highly auspicious*, *Kusuma Sanchaya Sutra*, and so on. Among these books, *The Handing Down of Buddha's Teachings* co-translated by Tanyao and Kekaya who is a master of Tripitaka come from Western Region was the most influential one. This book comprehensively told the promotion history of Indian Buddhism. It listed successive inheritors of Indian Buddhist teachings for the first time, such as Shakya, Kashyapa, Ananda, Shanavasa, Upagupta, Dhritaka, Mikkaka, Buddhanandi, Buddhamitra, Parshva, Punyayashas, Ashvaghosha, Pila, Nagarjuna, Kanadeva, Rahula, Sanghanandi, Sanghayashas, Kumaralata, Jayata, Vasubandhu, Manura, Haklena (Haklenayasas) and Aryasimha. Japanese scholars Sekino Tadashi and Tokiwa Daijo wrote in *Shanxi Datong* (translated by Zhao Yide): "Tanyao's spirit of carrying on the teachings of Buddhism have been

1 some res
and move
2 unit of
Northern
lent to m
译者注
3 the direc
4 Wenche

completely inherited by Lingyu in the Sui Dynasty. 24 inheritors who carried on the buddhist doctrine after the death of Shakyamuni were carved on the inner Wall of Baoshan Grottoes excavated by Lingyu, which is an imitation of the 24 inheritors recorded in *The Handing Down of Buddha's Teachings*. There are also many inheritors after Lingyu." We believed that Tanyao's translation of *The Handing Down of Buddha's Teachingsis* the beginning of the idea for Buddhist master to pass on the lamp of Buddhist doctrine to his disciples in China. The popular methods of establishing a sect and transmitting Buddhist doctrines in various sects of Buddhism after the Tang Dynasty also originated from it.

f) *Avatamsaka Sutra* became popular

The excavation of Yungang Grottoes was a reflection of the gradual improvement of Chinese Buddhist ideological system. Sekino Tadashi and Tokiwa Daijo once said: "There is no doubt that Tanyao asked Emperor Wencheng to excavate the five caves for the five emperors after Emperor Taizu. Therefore, the five caves have the meaning of the temple of the five emperors' spirits... In this way, the eternal Buddhist arts have been generated under the coincidental integration between Tanyao's spirits of promoting Buddhism and the motivation of the Wei royal family to confess and pursue filial. The guidelines of creating Buddha statues are at least relevant with the story of Buddha's life and some Mahayana sutras such as *Lotus Sutra*, *Vimalakirti-nirdesha Sutra*, *Sutra of Golden Light*, *Amitayus Sutra and Maitreya Sutra*. The thoughts of Avatamsaka sutra are also in it." The 29th volume of *Sequel to Biographies of Eminent Monks* recorded the spread of *Avatamsaka Sutra* in Pingcheng: "In the early years of Tai-he, there was an eunuch who felt shame about the corporal punishment on his body, and thought he was inferior to the human race, so he begged the Emperor to allow him to practice Buddhism in mountains. The Emperor permitted his request. This eunuch had taken *Avatamsaka Sutra* with him, and diligently and persistently studied and read this sutra day and night. In the early summer, he returned to the mountains, he even had grown mustache like a real and complete man by the end of June. He recovered the face and manliness, which was reported to the Emperor. When the Emperor heard the news, his admiration for Buddhism doubled, so *Avatamsaka Sutra* started to be popular in Dai country. The story could also be found in Buddhist Paranormal Events written by Hou Junsu." About *Avatamsaka Sutra*, the Buddhist Zhi Faling had carried the foreign language version from Khotan to Central Plains, and the Hindu Dhyana master Buddhabhadra translated to Chinese version in Daochang Temple in Jiankang in 420. This sutra was unknown to the world for over half a century due to its numerous contents. After the formation of the Pingcheng Buddhist center, monks from all over the world came here. The study, chanting and teaching of this Mahayana sutra which named *Avatamsaka Sutra* became an academic research project and a hot science. Since then, the foundation for the prosperity of the *Avatamsaka* school and *Avatamsaka* science in Tang Dynasty has been laid.

g) The preaching of The *Four-Part Vinaya*

During the Northern and Southern Dynasties, Chinese monks abided by *Mahasanghika Vinaya*. The 23th volume of Sequel to *Biographies of Eminent Monks* wrote by Daoxuan in the Tang Dynasty recorded: "Although the translation of *The Four-Part Vinaya* of Dharmagupta school started in the Later Qin Dynasty, its preaching and popularity were in the Northern Wei Dynasty. It was first chanted by Chi-Zi-Lun-Zhu (Buddhayashas) in the Western Regions without being preached to the outside world. None of the monks studied it there. The study of it started under the impact of famous Buddhists such as Facong and Daofu.... The general popularity of *The Four-Part* school is now mistaken for a tradition of the Tang Dynasty....Since the beginning of the study of Vinaya discipline, the Buddhist master Facong was praised by the Northern Wei Emperor Xiaowen in Beitai, he preached *The Four-Part Vinaya* by word of mouth that was respected and honored by many people. The Buddhist Daofu inherited Facong's career, formed a six-volume text on this sutra. The content of it includes long text but no behavior guide. However, for Buddhist monks at that time, the Buddhist doctrine of this text version is pure. Therefore, they all followed *The FourPart Vinaya* without distractions. At the end of the Wei Dynasty and the beginning of the Northern Qi Dynasty, the Buddhist Huiguang received the guidance of the master Bhadra who considered it necessary to understand the Buddhist teachings before annotating them and then categorizing them. Preaching and learning like gathering clouds were everywhere, popularizing the teachings of the Vinaya to a climax, made the shine of it being like the sun and moon. Every time they explained publicly, would be thousands of monks there. They discussed with each other and expressed their opinions, engraved it in volumes and named after various factions... Among those who preached in Dongchuan or in the south, even the most excellent ones were not as good as monks in the capital of Wei." Notes: Chi-Zi-Lun-Zhu referred to the Buddhist monk Buddhayashas who came from Kubha and chanted *The Four-Part Vinaya* in the Later Qin Dynasty; Facong and Daofu are the Buddhist master of Vinaya in Pingcheng in the Northern Wei Dynasty governed by Emperor Xiaowen; Bhadra, a Hindu monk, first set up Chan monasteries in Pingcheng, excavated stones as niche, then set up Shaolin monastery in Luoyang. Huiguang was an apprentice of Bhadra. In this way, *The Four-Part Vinaya* was translated in Chang'an in the Later Qin Dynasty, first developed in Pingcheng of the Northern Wei Dynasty, then got famous in the Northern Qi and became popular in the Tang Dynasty. The contribution of Pingcheng Buddhism in the aspect of Vinaya-pitaka was obvious.

To sum up, the formation and establishment of Chinese Buddhism Center in Pingcheng in the Northern Wei Dynasty is a significant milestone in the history of Chinese Buddhism. Its historical position and effect of continuing with the past and opening up the future cannot be underestimated. Moreover, the impacts of Pingcheng Buddhism and arts on Koguryo and Japan are also gradually known to people worldwide.

个子平

关于云冈石窟的著作不计其数，而本书则以大画幅黑白胶片摄影的视角，重新阐释之。

摄影视角下的云冈，不乏其有。1907 年至 1908 年间，法国的东方研究专家沙畹，将其摄制的石窟照片收入《华北考古学使命记》中。1938 年至 1944 年间，日本学者水野清一、长广敏雄率领的京都大学调查队对石窟进行了七次调查，并对第 8 窟至第 13 窟、第 14 窟至第 20 窟的窟前地面与山顶佛寺遗址，进行了考古发掘，并将其摄影、实测、线描、拓片、论文等成果结集为 16 卷、32 本之巨的专著《云冈石窟》，1951 年至 1956 年间陆续出版。

云冈摄影的兴起，当然源于摄影术的发明，但与各类文字报告也息息相关。1902 年 6 月，日本学者伊东忠太等在中国进行考察旅行，无意中发现了石窟建筑群，随后发表的《云冈旅行记》《山西云冈石窟寺》引起学术界的注意与兴趣，中外学者由此开启了云冈石窟的研究。之后，一批批的日本学者直奔此地而来。1915 年，大村西崖的《支那美术史·雕塑篇》出版；1919 年，松本文三郎的《支那佛教遗物》出版；1921 年，木下杢太郎、木村庄八的《大同石佛寺》出版；1921 年，山本明的《云冈石窟》出版，1924 年，山本明的另一部作品《震旦旧迹图汇第一编·云冈石窟》出版；1925 年，中井宗太郎解说、外村氏摄影的《大同石佛大观》出版；1926 年，常盘大定、关野贞的《支那文化史迹》出版。

自京绥铁路开通，云冈石窟即成为国内文人游学的热点，他们留下过大量日记游记、考察报告，如 1915 年王耀成的《大同游记》、1919 年陈垣的《记大同武州山石窟寺》、1919 年袁希涛的《大同云冈石窟佛像记》、1921 年瞿兑之的《大同游记》、1923 年吴新吾的《大同云冈游记及其感想》、1931 年丰子恺的《云冈石窟》、1933 年顾颉刚的《大同观感》、1934 年陈赓雅的《大同活泼地与大佛寺》、1934 年谢国桢的《大同石窟寺》等等，不一而足。这些文章，或解析云冈历史，或介绍邻邦研究成果，成为云冈石窟艺术形式与艺术来源的探索之作。

1933 年 9 月，林徽因、梁思成来到石窟考察。他们来到石窟，眼前一片荒凉，连住宿的旅馆也找不到，只好在一家农户的一间连门窗都没有的屋子里住了三天。此时的气候更让其难以忍受。午炎热，晚寒冷，吃的当然只能凑合，土豆与玉米面糊糊已算不错。他们每天不顾风吹日晒，爬到石窟顶端进行测绘，坚持将石窟的建筑艺术作了系统记录，且很快写出了论文《云冈石窟中所表现的北魏建筑》，发表在《中国营造学社汇刊》1933 年 12 月第 3 卷第 3、4 期上。该文运用比较研究的方法对石窟做了三方面的研究：一是石窟建造的年代、布置、构造；二是石窟中所表现的北魏建筑物；三是石窟中飞仙的雕刻及雕饰花纹的题材、样式等。还将云冈石窟与敦煌莫高窟、印度洞窟，以及希腊、日本的建筑艺术作比较，得出如此结论：

> 云冈石窟所表现的建筑式样，大部为中国固有的方式，并未受外来多少影响，不但如此，且使外来物同化于中国，塔即其例……在结构根本原则及形式上，中国建筑二千年来保持其独立性，不曾被外来影响所动摇。所谓受印度希腊影响者，实仅限于装饰雕刻两方面的。……在雕刻上只强烈地触动了中国雕刻艺术的新创造——其精神，气魄，格调，根本保持着中国固有的。而最后却在装饰花纹上，输给中国以大量的新题材、新变化、新刻法，散布流传直至今日，的确是个值得注意的现象。

1934 年，正在燕京大学女子文理学院任教的冰心女士来到云冈石窟，陪同者是一位姓吴的骑兵营长。他们“自大同车站出发……沿着泥泞颠簸的山路，汽车徐徐的开向武州山，沿途傍武州河而行，河水浑浊汹涌，时见人畜绝流而渡”。经过一座被称为观音堂的小庙，上阶入庙，庙内驻着军队，大殿内纵横设着兵士的卧具，神像的两目被黄纸蒙上，以避不便。吴营长为冰心指点对面山顶上的马武寨，那里据传是马武为盗时啸聚之处，他对冰心说：“这里静极了，夜里只听见水澌和狼叫。”冰心在 7 月 11 日的日记中写道：

> 向东而行，入别墅东第一窟，土气触鼻，从人以束香高照，鸦鸽惊起，从我们顶上纷纷飞出。在洞中暮色迷茫之下，我瞻仰了第一处云冈的造像。当中一尊坐佛高六丈许，旁有两大佛侍立，腰以下，已见剥损，法相庄严，默然外望，对于千数百年来窟外宇宙之流转变迁，在美妙慧澈的目光中，似不起什么感触。

“万亿化身，罗刻满山，鬼斧神工，骇人心目”，冰心总结她的云冈石窟游历，“目不能注，足不能停，如偷儿骤入宝窟，神魂丧失，莫知所携，事后追忆亦如梦入天宫”。

法国人沙畹用照相机留下了那个时代的石窟图像。照片中，石窟荒凉颓败，门无蹄辙，残破的断墙，衰败的庭院，一位老农腰系草绳，衣着褴褛，形容憔悴，他背后还有一些农民，正把羊和猪往洞窟里赶。冰心盛赞“鬼斧神工”的石窟，当时却被村民用作饲养猪羊的圈舍。

并非专家讲道，我只谈术，摄影的出现，是一场视觉革命，是另一门类的记录，摄影对历史具有塑造性，多了一幅摄影，便多了一个世界。也许是沙畹的镜头起了作用，1973 年，法国总统蓬皮杜访华，指名要求参观云冈石窟，9 月 15 日，周恩来总理陪同其前来参观。

本书的两位摄影人赵富义与宫品仁，采用的是大画幅黑白胶片摄影，可谓起步晚而起点高。如今已进入数码时代，其仍采用传统方式为之，自是别有心意。大画幅胶片摄影有着独到的表现方式、呈相特点，保持了一种静观世界的态度，而又透露着无以言表的含蓄。好的摄影作品，不仅感受客观，且具视觉张力，感知的差异化与矛盾化程度越高，冲击性便越强，由此能够开启读者的注意力视窗。视觉媒介激活读者，图像通过视觉聚焦，可与读者产生互动，摄影师为读者提供融入故事、置身画内的主观体验，使之感同身受，进而引发共鸣。

一缕霞光，一抹斜阳，从万头攒动的地标，到无人问津的角落，好的摄影作品，用热爱拍就，他们无数次走近石窟，又无数次经历反复，以期达到专业与表现的极限。为适应当代读者对视觉的无限欲求，便须挑战视觉，超越视觉，使之专美，这正是两位摄影人的诚心所在。视觉是人类的基本感知能力，观看先于言语，世界不仅仅是眼前的模样，还具图像的视觉意义——你所看到的画面，乃由内心取向投射的影像。久蓄胸中，触机而发，镜头定格时间的刹那，他们足足用了十年。

摄影不只是文字的伴手礼，也可独立成篇。作为云冈石窟精神共同体的重要组成部分，你无法定义某个瞬间的价值，直至其成为经典后才可以。但愿如此，但愿如此。

ie Ziping

There have already been countless publications on the Yungang Grottoes. This new contribution is presented from the perspective of large format black and white film photography and aims to shed some new light on the subject.

Illustrations of the Yungang Grottoes with photography have been numerous. As early as 1908, French sinologist Édouard Chavannes had published his photographs of the grottoes in *Mission archeologique dans la Chine septentrionale (Archaeological Mission to Northern China)*. During 1938 through 1944, Japanese scholars Mizuno Seiichi and Nagahiro Toshio led the Mission of the Tohobunka Kenkyusho (Institute of Oriental Culture) of Kyoto University to Yungang Grottoes and conducted seven investigations, and excavated the sites in front of Cave No.8-13 and Cave No.14-20, as well as the hilltop site of a Buddhist monastery ruins. All their findings and results, including photographs, drawings, survey plans, rubbings and essays were compiled into a monumental sixteen-volume, thirty-two-book publication: *Yun-Kang: the Buddhist Cave-temples of the Fifth Century A.D. in North China*, which had been published gradually from 1951 through 1956.

Thanks not only to the invention of photography, but also various kinds of textual reports on Yungang, we have witnessed a thriving interest in these ancient grottoes. At its start point, it was the Japanese architect Ito Chuta who first noticed these cave temples during his travel and research in China, and the following publications of his travelogue and a report on Yungang Grottoes attracted attentions and the subsequent focused researches of the academic circles. Other Japanese scholars are the first dispatch: Omura Seigai published his *Shina bijutsu shi Choso hen (History of Chinese Art: Sculpture Edition)* in 1915; Matsumoto Bunzaburo's *Shina bukkyo ibutsu (Buddhist Remains in China) in 1919*; Kinoshita Mokutaro and Kimura Shohachi's *Daido sekibutsuji (Datong Cave Temples)* and Yamamoto Akira's *Unko sekkutsu (Rock-carvings from the Yun-kang Caves)* in 1921; in 1924, Yamamoto Akira had another publication coming out: *Shintan kyuuseki zui Unko sekkutsu (A Pictorial Collection of Chinese Ancient Sites: the Yun-Kang Caves); in 1925 Daido sekibutsu tenbo (The Great View of Datong Stone Buddhas)* photographed by Mr. Sotomura and commented by Nakai Sotaro was published; Tokiwa Daijo and Sekino Tadashi published their *Shina bunka shiseki (Chinese Cultural Heritage)* in 1926.

Since the opening of the Peiping-Suiyuan Railway, the Yungang Grottoes have become a hot spot for domestic literati's academic travels. They have left a large number of travel notes, diary entries as well as academic reports - for examples "Travel Notes to Datong" by Wang Yaocheng in 1915, "On the Wuzhoushan Cave Temples of Datong" by Chen Yuan and "On the Buddhist Statues of Yungang Grottoes of Datong" by Yuan Xitao, both in 1919; "Travel Notes to Datong" by Qu Duizhi in 1921; "Travel Notes and Reflections on Datong Yungang Grottoes" by Wu Xinwu in 1923; "Yungang Grottoes" by Feng Zikai in 1931; "Perceptions of Datong" by Gu Jiegang in 1933; "Datong the Lively Land and Big Buddha Temple" by Chen Gengya in 1934; "Datong Cave Temples" by Xie Guozhen in 1934, and so on. These articles either analyze the history of Yungang or introduce the research results of neighboring countries, and thus constitute an early explorative sample of researches into the origins and art forms of Yungang Grottoes.

In September 1933, Lin Huiyin and Liang Sicheng visited the grottoes. When they came, they saw a desolate and disserted place without even a travel lodge to find, so they settled in a peasant's shack with no doors or windows for three days. The climate at the time made the situation even more unbearable: hot in the day and cold in the evening. Food was of course just make-do, with potatoes and cornmeal batter deemed as rare decent meals. Regardless of the challenging situation, they climbed high up in the grottoes every day to conduct surveying and mapping, and systematically recorded the architectural aspects of the grottoes, and soon published an essay titled "The Architecture of the North Wei Dynasty as Revealed in the Yung-Kang Grottoes" in Volume 4, Issues 3&4 of *Bulletin of the Society for Research in Chinese Architecture* in June 1934. The essay uses the comparative methods to study three aspects of the grottoes: firstly, the dating, layout and tectonic structure of the grottoes; secondly, the style of the North Wei architecture as represented in the grottoes; and thirdly, the carving patterns and styles of flying immortals and other decorative motifs in the grottoes. It also compares the Yungang Grottoes with the Dunhuang Mogao Grottoes, the Indian cave arts, and the ancient Greek and Japanese architecture, then comes to this conclusion:

> *"Most of the architectural styles shown in the Yungang Grottoes are inherently Chinese and barely indicate any influence from outside. Not only that, they also demonstrate assimilations and Sinicizations of foreign objects, with pagoda as one good example... In terms of the fundamental principles of structure and form, Chinese architecture has maintained its independence for two millennia and not been shaken by foreign influences. The so-called influences by India and Greece are in fact only limited to the two aspects of decoration and sculpture... In terms of sculpture, they have only triggered a strong new wave of innovation and creation in Chinese sculptural art, yet its spirit, vigor and style are still inherently Chinese. But in the end, in terms of decorative patterns and motifs, they did export a large number of new themes, new changes and new methods into China, which have been widely spreading and proliferating till this day. It is indeed a phenomenon worth notifying."*

In 1934, Mme. Bing Xin, who was teaching at the Women's College of Yenching University at the time, visited the Yungang Grottoes, accompanied by a cavalry battalion commander named Wu. They "set off from Datong Station...along the muddy and bumpy mountain road, and along the turbid and turbulent Wuzhou River, the car slowly drove towards Wuzhou Mountain. Now and then, there were people and livestock seen crossing the river." When passing by a small temple called Guanyin Hall, they climbed up the steps and entered the temple. There were troops stationed in the temple. Soldiers' beddings were laid out all over in the main hall, therefore the eyes of all the statues in the hall were covered with yellow paper to avoid blasphemy. Battalion Commander Wu pointed out the hilltop Mawuzhai Village across the river, which was said to be the place where Ma Wu gathered his fellows when he was a bandit. He said to Mme. Bing Xin: "It is very quiet here. At night, I only hear the rushing water and the howling of wolves." In the July 11 entry of her diary, Bing Xin wrote:

> *"Walking eastward, we entered the first cave to the east of the villa. The scent of earth rushed into our noses. The retinues burnt some incense sticks, while a flock of crows and pigeons were startled to fly out from above us. In the twilight, I paid homage to the first Yungang statues in the cave. The sitting Buddha in the center is about sixty feet high, flanked by two huge standing Buddhas which have been weathered below the waist. But the dignified and solemn look of the Buddhas remain. They look outwards from inside the grotto in total silence, upon the flows and changes of the universe outside for thousands of years, which seem to arouse nothing, and nothing to be felt in these wonderful and lucid gazes."*

"With trillions of incarnations carved all over the mountain, the uncanny craftsmanship shocked and shook the average eyes and minds", Mme. Bing Xin summed up her trip to the Yungang Grottoes, "My eyes not being able to focus, feet not being able to stop, I was like a thief stumbling into a treasure cave, dazzled and confused, wondering about what to carry, and eventually came out empty-handed, only to remember it afterwards like a wild dream into the heavenly palace."

But Édouard Chavannes' camera captured a glimpse of the grottoes of that time. The grottoes in the photo are desolate and decadent, surrounded by a decaying courtyard with broken walls. An old peasant in ragged clothes, with a haggard face and a grass rope tied around his waist, stands in the courtyard. Behind him are some other peasants who are busy driving sheep and pigs into the grottoes. Mme. Bing Xin praised the "uncanny craftsmanship" of the art in the grottoes, but at the time she visited, they were used by villagers as pens for raising pigs and sheep.

I'm not qualified as an expert preaching on the art and only interested in photography as a technique. The emergence of photography was a visual revolution. It constructed a new type of documentation, and thus participated in restructuring history. Every photograph constructs a specific perspective to see the world. Perhaps inspired by Chavannes' images, in his state visit to China in 1973, French President Georges Pompidou specifically requested to pay a visit to the Yungang Grottoes. On September 15 of the year, Premier Zhou Enlai accompanied him on the trip.

The two photographers featured in this publication, Zhao Fuyi and Gong Pinren, use large format black and white film to do photography. This is what is called "starting late but starting high". In this advanced digital age by which we are totally overwhelmed, the choice of a traditional technology and method is certainly deliberate. Large-format film photography has a unique way of expression and representation, maintaining an attitude of quietly observing the world, while revealing an indescribable implicitness. Excellent photography not only touches upon the objective, but also creates visual tension. The higher the degree of differentiation and contradiction in perception, the more powerful the impact feels, and the more easily it can attract the viewer's attention. Visual media activates the viewer, and images interact with the viewer through visual focus; the photographer provide the viewer with a subjective experience of being integrated into the frame and the story, so that the viewer can empathize and resonate. Be it a touch of afterglow, a swipe of setting sunlight, a popular landmark or an unknown corner, excellent photography works with passion and love. The photographers in this case have approached the grottoes countless times, and reworked on their oeuvres countless times, in order to get real close to the professional limit. Also, in order to fulfil contemporary viewers' infinite appetite for visual spectacles, it is necessary to challenge the limit of visual performance and try to transcend it. This is where the sincerity of the two photographers shows. Vision is one of the basic perceptive abilities of human beings. It precedes speech. The world is not just what you see, but has meanings – it reflects your inner dispositions through the image you capture. The photographers waited ten years for the moments when the opportunity struck, and their cameras captured the moments. Photography is not just a companion to the text; it could make a statement itself, independently.

As an important part of the spiritual community of Yungang Grottoes, the value of the documentation of a specific moment cannot be decided until it becomes a classic. Or not. And I surely hope for the former, sincerely.

第 1 窟（石鼓洞）公元 471—494 年　第 1、2 窟为一组塔庙双窟，窟外两侧各残存一座单层方塔。第 1 窟外壁明窗东侧题刻清代朱廷翰《游云冈石佛寺诗》。窟内平面呈长方形，平顶，中央方塔上下两层，仿木构屋顶塔檐。塔顶处蛟龙盘绕，须弥山逶迤。北壁主像为交脚弥勒菩萨。东壁下层浮雕“睒子本生”故事。据考证，第 1、2 窟辽代以前建为护国寺，为云冈十寺之一。明清号曰“石鼓寒泉”，属云中八景之一。

第 2 窟（寒泉洞）公元 471—494 年　窟外壁明窗上方及西侧题刻“山水有清音”“云深处”。窟内三级方塔居中，塔面上刻出瓦筒、檐椽、斗拱等仿木建筑构件，上层四角镂刻八角柱。窟内四壁分层分段布局，最上层雕刻天宫伎乐列龛，下面依次为锯齿纹垂幔带、禅定坐佛带、大型列龛、长卷式浮雕故事，最下层为供养人列像。北壁主像为释迦坐佛，风化严重。东壁下层浮雕太子“箭射铁鼓”佛传故事。该窟地下有泉水涌出，旧名“寒泉洞”。

第 3 窟（灵岩寺洞）　公元 471—494 年　云冈最大的洞窟，原设计为大型塔庙窟，但终北魏一代未能完成。窟外依崖原建有木构大阁，今仅存上方一排 12 个梁孔，说明当年的佛阁为面阔十一开间巨制。上层台面两端各一座三级方塔，两塔间凿二明窗，明窗之间为一庑殿形窟室，主像雕交脚弥勒。窟面东西各开一门，窟内北壁雕阿弥陀佛、观世音和大势至菩萨三尊像，即“西方三圣”。主尊阿弥陀佛高 10 米，倚坐，面部圆润丰满，神态超然。两侧菩萨头戴宝冠，精美庄严。其雕凿年代，目前有北魏、隋、唐及辽四说，多依据造像艺术风格而推论。窟内留下的分割、揭取岩石的遗迹，是了解古代石窟开凿方法的珍贵实物资料。

第 5 窟（大佛洞）公元 471—494 年　第 5、6 窟为一组双窟，窟前四层木构楼阁为清初顺治八年（1651）宣大总督佟养量主持修建，因岩结构，蔚为壮观。即明代云中八景中的“云冈摩云”。窟门两壁上层各雕一株枝繁叶茂的圣树，二佛侧身树下对坐，神情安详；下层金刚力士头戴双翼羽冠，身穿甲胄，威风凛凛。窟内北壁坐佛高 17 米，是云冈石窟中最高大的佛像，后世包泥彩绘，呈唐代风格。东西两壁各一立佛，西立佛鼻直眉弯，略显笑意，雍容秀典。后壁凿有礼拜道。

第 6 窟（释迦佛洞）　公元 471—494 年　该窟为中心柱窟，亦名支提窟、塔庙窟，雕饰富丽，被誉为“云冈第一伟观”，是世界雕刻艺术史上的奇迹。窟内中央方形塔柱分上下层，高 15 米。上层四面各镌一立佛二菩萨，四角镂雕大象承驮九级楼阁式方塔；下层四面开龛坐佛。窟内四壁上层环列立佛十一尊，华盖承悬，气宇轩昂。窟顶格状，格间可见骑乘孔雀、狮子、虎、长尾鸟等动物的多臂多首天神。窟内现存反映释迦一生的佛传故事图 30 余幅，集中表现了佛主从诞生、成长、婚姻，到出家、弘法等一系列具有标志性纪念意义的场面。这些故事图雕刻，结构合理，手法简朴，为犍陀罗艺术东传的新创造，弥足珍贵。

第 7 窟（西来第一佛洞）　公元 471—494 年　第 7、8 窟是云冈最早的双窟。窟具前后室，主室平面呈横长方形。窟内造像胡风汉韵，交相杂糅，东西文化在这里发生了最绚烂的撞击与交融。第 7 窟明窗两壁为比丘树下参禅思惟像。北壁上层大龛正中为交脚弥勒菩萨，两侧为倚坐佛像，下层为释迦、多宝二佛并坐。南壁长方形帷幕龛内，六身高发髻供养天半跪相对，端静秀丽，风姿绰约，素有“云冈六美人”之誉，是西域造像融入东方元素的上乘之作。窟顶摹仿木构建筑中的平棊藻井，24 对飞天围绕盛开的莲花飘然曼舞。

第 8 窟（佛籁洞）　公元 471—494 年　窟门西侧雕骑乘孔雀的鸠摩罗天，五头六臂，颜若童子，踏发喜笑，手中或托举日月，或执弓箭，左下手当胸持斑鸠。具有浓郁的异域风情。东侧骑神牛的摩醯首罗天，三头八臂，面型浑圆，两侧小头戴尖顶帽，主臂一手叉腰，一手持谷穗，其余支臂或托日月，或执弓箭，或提如意。多首多臂天神像造型来源于古印度，原为婆罗门教神祇。该组雕像为云冈石窟所独有，反映了早期佛教杂密兼容的特征。

第 9 窟（阿閦佛洞）　公元 471—494 年　第 9 ～ 13 窟俗称“五华洞”，因后世施泥彩绘而异常绚丽。这组洞窟营造于北魏民族变革、文化更新的时代，窟像汉风转浓，具有鲜明的中国化、民族化特色。第 9、10 窟为一组双窟，前后室结构，汉式殿堂布局。窟门列楹柱，面各三间。柱雕千佛，承以狮、象，蔚为壮观。第 9 窟窟门为仿中国传统庑殿式建筑，两侧对称布龛，分层雕刻，中西合璧，具有浓重的装饰意味。窟内四壁分层布龛，造像题材多出自《法华经》。窟顶格状，格内雕团莲及飞天，八夜叉体魄健硕，力举万钧，单手承托横枋。后室北壁主像雕释迦，东西两壁各一胁侍菩萨。

第 10 窟（毗卢佛洞）　公元 471—494 年　前室北壁明窗与拱门之间，须弥山层峦叠嶂，山腰二龙交缠，山间有茂密的林木和竞奔的动物。外侧，阿修罗天单腿盘坐，多头多臂，手托日月。东西两壁各雕三间式屋形龛，龛内佛像面相慈和，菩萨神情恬静。阎浮树下，半跏坐思惟菩萨，一手支颐，沉于四谛。窟门东西两侧金刚力士，头戴鸟羽冠，手持金刚杵，表情和善。后室主像为弥勒菩萨，东西两壁各一胁侍菩萨。南壁为表现释迦因施善教、降服外道的因缘故事龛。

第 11 窟（接引佛洞）　公元 471—494 年　第 11、12、13 窟为一组。第 11 窟内中心塔柱上下两层，样式朴拙简约。下层四面均一立佛，正面立佛两侧另有二胁侍菩萨，细颈瘦腰，神态温雅，为辽代补凿。西壁屋形大龛内七立佛，波状发式，面型丰润，形体高大，华衣飘逸。东壁上层太和七年（483）造像题铭，全文共 337 字，是云冈石窟现存时间最早、文字最多的题记，书体端朴高古，寄巧于拙，是平城魏碑书法的精品。窟内四壁龛制纷杂，无统一规制，约系北魏民间集资续凿。

第 12 窟（离垢地菩萨洞）　公元 471—494 年　俗称“音乐窟”。前后窟室，前室外壁上方凿窟檐，窟口列楹柱。前室北壁最上层天宫伎乐十四身，分别演奏吹指、齐鼓、排箫、琵琶、横笛、琴、五弦、筚篥、箜篌、腰鼓、义嘴笛、法螺等乐器。门楣上一组舞伎群，动作连贯，气韵奔放，是人间舞姿的艺术再现。窟顶逆发形伎乐天，体格壮硕，具有北方少数民族性格特点。该窟内乐器雕刻的形制、演奏方式以及乐队的组合形式，集中体现了北魏宫廷乐队风貌和社会音乐制度，是研究中国古代音乐史的珍贵资料。

第 13 窟（文殊菩萨洞）　公元 471—494 年　穹窿窟顶，主像为交脚弥勒菩萨，高 13 米，头戴宝冠，颈部戴悬铃项圈及璎珞，胸佩蛇饰，双肩唧珠。右手臂肘下，一力士四臂奋力托举，势若拔山。该像经后代包泥彩绘，原雕仅见双足踏莲。东壁龛像，殿堂飞阁，流苏帷帐，神龙跃动，尽显汉风。南壁明窗与窟门之间屋形大龛内，七立佛造像气韵高雅。

第 14 窟　公元 494—525 年　窟分前后室，历经渗水侵蚀，雕像风化剥蚀严重，南壁及部分窟顶旧已坍塌，仅东千佛柱残存。窟口两立柱为 1994 年依旧恢复。西壁下层方形龛内，左维摩，右文殊，正中一立菩萨，右手托钵、左手执莲，表现的是《维摩诘经》中“观众生品”的故事内容。

第 15 窟（万佛洞）　公元 494—525 年　方形单窟室，以表现千佛题材为主，旧称“千佛洞”。窟内现存造像逾万，故又称“万佛洞”。这些象征释迦分身的十方化佛，排列有序，构图严谨。西壁盝形帷幕龛基博山炉两侧，雕刻鱼鸟水藻，呈现出沙鸥翔集、鱼跃于渊的自然景致。下方龛额伎乐飞天，天衣灵动，缥缈若仙，飞翔的态势与上方波动的水草，韵律谐合。

第 16 窟（立佛洞）　公元 460—470 年　第 16—20 窟是云冈最早开凿的一组洞窟，因系著名高僧昙曜主持营建，故称“昙曜五窟”。窟制相同，平面呈马蹄形，穹窿顶，窟内造像以三世佛为主，主像雕饰奇伟，冠于一世，分别象征着北魏的五位皇帝。第 16、17 窟是一组。第 16 窟主像为释迦立佛，高 13.5 米，波纹状发髻，清秀俊逸。佛像身穿褒衣博带式袈裟，胸前结带下垂，属北魏太和年间推行汉化时的服制。

第 17 窟（弥勒三尊洞）　公元 460-470 年　主像是菩萨装的交脚弥勒，高 15.6 米，头戴宝冠，胸佩蛇饰及短璎珞，臂着钏，斜披络腋，束腰收腹，下穿羊肠长裙，狮子座，具有浓郁的异域情调。西壁立佛面庞浑圆，造型古朴壮美。东壁坐佛双肩齐挺，服饰线条流畅，刀法娴熟。窟内四壁以千佛雕刻为主，雕像清简劲直，纯真朴质，反映了云冈早期造像的艺术特点。西壁佛像背光外缘供养天，单腿半跪，双手捧莲，神情恬静，造型优美。明窗东壁太和十三年（487）造像龛，是云冈石窟分期断代的重要标尺。

第 18 窟（立三佛洞）　公元 460—470 年　第 18、19、20 窟为一组，第 19 窟是中心窟，开凿时间最早。第 18 窟设计严谨，布局完整，北壁主佛像高 15.5 米，高肉髻，面颊丰圆，鼻梁高挺，浑厚质朴，身披千佛袈裟，两侧分别配置胁侍佛、胁侍菩萨及十大弟子像。左胁佛头顶华盖，面庞浑圆，体魄伟岸。左胁菩萨头戴花冠，秀丽典雅。上端五弟子雕刻，俱为西域人特征，或提瓶静立，或拈花微笑，或闭目倾听，或若有所悟，或喜从心生，鬼斧神工，令人叹绝。

第 19 窟（宝生佛洞） 公元 460—470 年 主佛像结跏趺坐，高 16.8 米，是云冈石窟中第二大佛。佛像耳轮齐肩，下颌崩毁。举右手肘下有一小柱支撑。衣纹简洁明快，轻薄贴体，袈裟边饰折带纹。南壁罗睺罗因缘是云冈最早的佛教故事图像。窟外东西各开一耳洞，内一倚坐佛像。这种分窟安置三世佛的布局设计，既有变化，又显庄严，是北朝石窟形制的新创举。前壁原有拱门与明窗，约与第 20 窟前壁同时坍塌。

第 20 窟（白佛爷洞） 公元 460—470 年 窟前立壁与窟顶早年崩塌，辽时建有木构窟檐，后毁于兵火，形成露天造像。主佛高 13.7 米，高肉髻，广额丰颐，长目高鼻，有八字髭，手结禅定印，质地厚重的袒右袈裟，衣纹凸起，具有犍陀罗造像遗风。大佛挺拔健硕的身躯，气势雄浑的神情，突出表现了鲜卑游牧民族的强大，是云冈石窟雕刻艺术的代表与象征，也是中国早期佛教雕刻艺术的空前杰作。大佛两侧各一立佛与胁侍菩萨，西像惜毁。

第 21-45 窟（西部诸窟） 公元 494—525 年 公元 494 年孝文帝迁都洛阳后，云冈石窟大规模的皇家开凿工程告停，民间开窟造像之风继起，一直延续到孝明帝正光年间。晚期洞窟以中小型洞窟居多，类型复杂，式样多变。四壁三龛及三壁重龛窟是这一时期流行的样式，造像题材以三世佛，释迦弥勒、释迦多宝二佛以及文殊维摩等组合较为常见。佛像一律褒衣博带，清秀俊逸；菩萨披帔帛，细颈削肩；飞天身材修长，长裙裹足。龛楣、帐饰日益繁杂，中国佛教造像艺术全面走向中国化、世俗化，并成为龙门石窟开凿的样本。

Cave 1 (Cave of Stone Drum) 471-494 CE Caves 1 and 2 have similar layout and make a pair, each containing a central pillar and therefore termed "chaitya" cave. On the outside, there is a seriously weathered single-story pagoda on each side of the entrance wall. To the east of the small window perching above the entrance archway is a Qing dynasty inscription of tourist poem by Zhu Tinghan: *On the Visit of Yungang Cave Temples*. The cave has a rectangular plan, flat roof and a central pillar in the form of a two-story square pagoda with pseudo-wooden eaves and roof. The end of the pagoda is coiled by dragons and topped by Mount Sumeru. The central statue on the north wall is a cross-ankled Maitreya Bodhisattva. The lower portion of the east wall depicts in relief the Jataka tale of Syama. According to scholars' research, before Liao Dynasty Caves 1 and 2 were initially part of a realm-protecting monastery built under imperial decree, which also belonged to a series of ten monasteries in Yungang. During Ming and Qing Dynasties, the two caves were also called "Cave of Stone Drum" and "Cave of Cold Spring", respectively. Each was hailed as one of the eight scenic spots in Datong area.

Cave 2 (Cave of Cold Spring) 471-494 CE To the west of and above the upper window on the outside wall are two inscriptions: "The mountains and rivers have clear sounds" and "Deep in the Clouds". The central pillar is in the form of a three-story square pagoda with carved pseudo-wooden structures such as eaves and bracket sets. The upper stories have octagonal corner columns. The four sidewalls of the cave are each laid out in layers, with the uppermost portion carved out as a series of niches for celestial musicians, and followed downward in order by zigzag patterns of hanging curtains, a series of meditative sitting Buddhas, a series of large niches and narrative scenes in the form of a long scroll of reliefs. The bottom portion depicts donors and worshippers. The central statue on the north wall is a severely weathered Sakyamuni Buddha in seated position. The lower portion of the east wall depicts the biographical tale of pre-enlightenment Buddha as Prince Siddhartha shooting the iron drums with an arrow. There is a spring gushing out from the underground of the cave, which was formerly known as "Cave of Cold Spring" - Clear, cold spring used to be found within the cave, hence the name.

Cave 3 (Cave of Divine Rock) 471-494 CE The largest in Yungang, Cave 3 was originally intended as a "chaitya" type cave, but it was left unfinished till the end of North Wei. A magnificent wooden pavilion was once built upon the cliff face outside the cave, but only a row of twelve beam holes now remains – evidence that the perished pavilion used to be an eleven-bay huge structure. There is a three-story square pagoda at each end of the upper-level terrace, and two upper windows opened between the two pagodas. Between the windows is the upper-level cave, which houses a cross-ankled Maitreya Bodhisattva as its main statue. The main cave is at the lower level, with two entrance gateways on both the east and west sides. In the cave three statues are seated next to the north wall, with Amitabha Buddha in the middle, flanked by Avalokitesvara and Mahasthamaprapta Bodhisattva on both sides - namely the "Amitabha Triad". The 10-meter-high main statue, Amitabha Buddha, is in throne-sitting position, with a plump round face and a detached demeanor. The flanking Bodhisattvas both wear jeweled crowns appearing exquisite and solemn. There are four theories about the dating of the statues mostly based on stylistic analysis: North Wei, Sui, Tang and Liao Dynasty. Traces of cutting and removal of rocks left in the cave are important evidences for understanding the technical aspects of ancient Buddhist grotto construction.

Cave 5 (Cave of Great Buddha) 471-494 CE Cave 5 makes a pair with the neighboring Cave 6. The four-story wooden pavilion built upon the rock face in front of the cave was constructed by Tong Yangliang, the early Qing dynasty Governor of Xuanfu and Datong, in the eighth year of Shunzhi Reign (1651). The place where it was built used to be hailed as one of the eight scenic spots in Datong area during Ming Dynasty: "Yungang Caressing Clouds". Carved on the upper portion of the side walls of the entrance gateway are two leafy bodhi trees, and two Buddhas are seated side by side under each tree, with peaceful expressions. The lower portion depicts a vajra warrior on each side, wearing double-winged feather crown and fully armored, looking majestic. The central Buddha seated next to the north wall of the cave is seventeen meters high, making it the tallest Buddha statue in the Yungang Grottoes. The stone sculpted statue was later covered with clay and painted in the style of Tang Dynasty. Flanking the central Buddha are two standing Buddhas, each on the side walls of the cave. The west wall standing Buddha shows a graceful appearance, with straight nose line and curved eyebrows and a subtle smile. Cut into the back wall of the cave is a circumambulatory passage used for worshipping the central Buddha.

Cave 6 (Cave of Sakyamuni Buddha) 471-494 CE Cave 6 is another cave with central pillar and called "chaitya cave". It is rich decorated with magnificent carvings, hailed as the "Yungang Spectacle", and none less than an artistic miracle in the history of world sculpture. The central pillar is carved in the form of a two-storied square pagoda, 15 meters high, with the upper level depicting a standing Buddha flanked by two Bodhisattvas on each side; an elephant carrying a nine-storied square pagoda at each corner; and a niche housing a seated Buddha on each side of the lower level. In the cave, there are eleven standing Buddhas circling the upper portion of the four walls, with canopies hanging above making the appearances majestic. The cave ceiling is coffered and decorated with multi-armed and multi-headed deities riding peacocks, lions, tigers, long-tailed birds and other animals. There are also more than 30 scenes from Sakyamuni Buddha's biographical tales, following a series of iconic and commemorative moments and stages of Buddha's life from birth, through coming of age, marriage, to departure from home, enlightenment and preaching Buddhism. The scenes are carved with concise techniques and thoughtful compositions. They are innovative localizations of the newly introduced Gandharan Buddhist art to the east and are of great importance.

Cave 7 (Cave of the First Buddha from the West) 471-494 CE Cave 7 and Cave 8 are the earliest twin caves in Yungang. The two caves both have a front and a back chamber, with the back chamber laid out in a horizontal rectangular plane. The statues in the caves show a mixture of Chinese and the Western Regions styles, with the two cultures confronting and exchanging with each other in a most splendid way. In Cave 7, on the side walls of the upper window are images of pensive Bhikkhus meditating under the tree. In the middle of the large niche on the upper portion of north wall is a cross-ankled Maitreya Bodhisattva flanked by seated Buddhas on both sides. The lower portion are occupied by Sakyamuni Buddha and Prabhuta-ratna Buddha seated sitting by side. In the rectangular niche with draped curtain on the south wall, six offering devas with tall buns are depicted in two groups facing each other in half-kneeling positions. They look quiet, beautiful and graceful, and have a reputation as the "Six Beauties of Yungang", deemed a masterpiece of sculptural art incorporating both the Western Regions techniques and oriental charms. The cave ceiling follows the style of coffered ceiling in wooden architecture, depicting in the grids twenty-four pairs of flying apsaras dancing gracefully around blooming lotuses.

Cave 8 (Cave of Buddha Sound) 471-494 CE Carved on the west wall of the entrance gateway is an image of five-headed and six-armed Kumara Deva riding a peacock. He appears as a boy wearing curling hair and a playful smile, exuding a strong exotic aura. In his six hands holding a sun and a moon, a bow and an arrow, and a turtledove in his lower left hand near his chest. On the east wall is a three-headed and eight-armed Maheshvara Deva riding a sacred cow. He has a round face, with the two side small heads wearing pointed hats. One of his main arms is on his waist, and the other is holding ears of grain. The other secondary arms are either holding a sun, a moon, or bows and arrows, or a ceremonial scepter. Images of the multi-headed and multi-armed gods originated from ancient India and were originally Brahman divinities. This group of statues is unique to the Yungang Grottoes, representing the characteristics of early esoteric Buddhism and its proliferation in north China.

Cave 9 (Cave of Akshobhya Buddha) 471-494 CE Cave 9-13 together used to be called Five Flower Caves by local people, because of the colorful painting inside the caves done by later generation artisans on an added coating of clay. The caves were originally constructed during North Wei dynasty, at a turning point of ethnic assimilation and cultural reformation. The statues in the cave have begun to show a more conspicuous Han Chinese influence from the South. Cave 9 and 10 are a pair, both laid out in a double-chamber plan with a Han Chinese temple hall arrangement. The entrance façades are divided by columns into three bays, with the Thousand-Buddha motif carved on each column, and each supported by a column base carved in motifs of lion or elephant. The overall visual effect is rather magnificent. Cave 9's façade also preserves a traditional Chinese hipped roof carved into the rock face above its entrance gateway, and niches are laid out in layers on both of its side walls, thus combining the Chinese architecture style with imported cave temple arts in a decorative yet harmonious way. Inside the cave, niches are arranged in layers on each of its side walls, and statues are sculpted mostly according to the Lotus Sutra. The coffered ceiling depicts apsara motifs and lotus patterns, and is supported by eight strong Yakshas single-handedly at the corners. Sakyamuni Buddha is the central statue on the north wall, while the east and west wall each accommodates an attendant Bodhisattva.

Cave 10 (Cave of Vairocana Buddha) 471-494 CE In the antechamber of Cave 10, between the north wall upper window and the entrance gateway, intertwined dragons are seen circling the Mount Sumeru, where dense forests and racing animals are also inhabiting. The multiple-headed-and-armed Asura Deva is sitting on the side in half-lotus position, holding a sun and a moon in his hands. There is a three-bay niche carved on each of the side walls, with meditative Buddhas and Bodhisattvas inside each niche. Under the Jambu tree, the half-lotus-seated pensive Bodhisattva supports his cheek with one hand and retreats himself in contemplating the Four Noble Truths. Two vajra warriors, wearing feathered crowns and calm expressions, stand holding vajras on each of the side walls of the entrance gateway. The central statue of the back chamber is a Maitreya Bodhisattva on the north wall and an attendant Bodhisattva on each of the side walls. The south wall contains a niche depicting scenes from Nidana tales such as Sakyamuni subduing and converting heretics with truthful teachings.

Cave 11 (Cave of Amitabha Buddha) 471-494 CE Cave 11, Cave 12 and Cave 13 make a group. The plain and simple central pillar in Cave 11 has two stories, with a standing Buddha carved on each side of the lower level, and the front side Buddha accompanied by two slim and elegant attendant Bodhisattvas added in Liao dynasty. A large temple-hall shaped niche on the west all houses seven standing Buddhas with wavy hair and plump face, all in tall figures and lavish robes. An inscription on the upper portion of east wall dated the seventh year of Taihe Reign (483) is the earliest extant inscription with the most characters (totaling 337 words) in the Yungang Grottoes. Its calligraphic style is one of simplicity and antiquity and of sophistication appearing as rusticity, making it a masterpiece of the Wei Stelae Calligraphy style from Datong the capital city of Wei. The niches on the walls of the cave are lacking an overall design, thus probably an outcome of a gradual construction process by the local believers throughout the North Wei dynasty.

Cave 12 (Cave of Vimala-Bhumi Bodhisattva) 471-494 CE Also called "Cave of Music" by local people, Cave 12 is arranged in a two-chamber layout. A pseudo-roof is carved out of the rock face outside the cave, supported by a series of eave columns at the entrance. The uppermost portion of the north wall of the antechamber depicts fourteen celestial musicians playing instruments like navel drum, panflute, *pipa*, flute, zither, five-string, *bili*, harp, *yizui* flute, waist drum, conch shell and so on or with their own fingers. A series of dancing performers depicted on top of the entrance gateway show coherent movement and unrestrained spirit, which is an artistic representation of the art of dance at the time. The celestial musician with reversed hairdressing on the cave ceiling shows a strong physique and characteristics of northern peoples. The illustration of musical instruments in Cave 12, the ways of performing these instruments as well as their orchestration embody the style of the court orchestra and socio-musical system of the North Wei dynasty. They are precious materials for studying the history of ancient Chinese music.

Cave 13 (Cave of Manjushri Bodhisattva) 471-494 CE Cave 13 has a domed ceiling. Its central statue is a cross-ankled Maitreya Bodhisattva thirteen meters in height, wearing a jeweled crown, a necklace with jewels and hanging bells and a snake ornament with double-heads-suckling-Mani-jewel motif on the chest. Beneath the elbow of his right arm is a guardian lifting it with all his four arms and strength, as if he is lifting a mountain. The statue was cladded with clay and color painted by later generation artisans, and only the two feet and the supporting lotus pedestals reveal the original North Wei craftsmanship. The statues in the niches on the east wall display unmistakable Han Chinese style with its soaring pavilions and palaces, hanging curtains and tassels, and dragons leaping and flying in between them. The large temple-hall shaped niche between the upper window and the entrance gateway on the south wall houses seven standing Buddhas with elegant charm.

Cave 14 494-525 CE The double-chambered Cave 14 has experienced serious water erosions during the past centuries, and its statues are mostly severely weathered. Part of the south wall and cave ceiling have collapsed, and only the east column with Thousand-Buddha motif remains. The eaves columns at the entrance were restored in 1994. The square niche on the lower portion of west wall depicts Vimalakirti on the left, Manjushri Bodhisattva on the right, and a standing Bodhisattva holding lotus flower and alms bowl in the middle, illustrating a scene from Chapter VII, "Viewing Sentient Beings", of *Vimalakirti Sutra*.

Cave 15 (Cave of Ten Thousand Buddhas) 494-525 CE Cave 15 has a square plan, and the Buddhist arts within mostly represent the Thousand-Buddha motif, hence the local name "Cave of Thousand Buddhas". But in actuality the cave is now preserving more than ten thousand Buddha images, therefore also called "Cave of Ten Thousand Buddhas". The Thousand-Buddha motif symbolizes countless incarnations of Buddha from all directions. They are arranged in a orderly fashion in the cave with a carefully controlled composition. On the west wall, besides the incense burner at the base of the truncated-tent shaped niche, motifs such as fish, birds and water plants are depicted to represent a natural scene of harmonious ecosystem. The lower portion of the niche illustrates celestial musicians and apsaras in agile and ethereal clothing, their flying posture echoing the undulating aquatic lives on the above.

Cave 16 (Cave of Standing Buddha) 460-470 CE Cave 16-20 are the earliest construction in Yungang, supposedly completed by the renown Monk Tan Yao, and therefore called the "Five Caves of Tan Yao". All of them are arranged in the same layout, with a hoof-shaped plane, domed ceiling, main statues mostly following the Tryadhva-Buddha theme. The main Buddha in each of the five caves is said to be representing a North Wei Emperor. Cave 16 and Cave 17 make a pair. The central Buddha in Cave 16 is a standing Sakyamuni Buddha 13.5 meters in height, with wavy hair and elegantly slim physique, wearing kasaya in the ample-gown-and-loose-girdle style with a knotted ribbon hanging down the chest, which is a clothing style typical of the Taihe period of North Wei dynasty when the movement of adopting Han Chinese culture was at its peak.

Cave 17 (Cave of Maitreya Triad) 460-470 CE The central statue of Cave 17 is a cross-ankled Maitreya Bodhisattva 15.6 meters in height, wearing a jeweled crown, short strings of jewels, arm bracelets, a snake ornament on the chest, a long scarf draped from the shoulder to waist and a long skirt, sitting on a lion-throne – all exuding a distinctively exotic charm. The standing Buddha on the west wall has a round face and a simple and strong figure. The seated Buddha on the east wall with straight shoulders and smooth clothing lines shows highly skilled craftsmanship. The walls behind the Buddha statues are mainly covered with Thousand-Buddha motifs, showing a pure and simple style explicating the characteristics of Yungang's early period of construction. The offering devas depicted on the edge of the aureola of the west wall Buddha are half kneeling and offering lotus to Buddha, with a peaceful facial expressions and graceful postures. The niche on the east wall of the upper window dated to the thirteenth year of Taihe Reign (487) is an important piece of evidence for periodization of the Yungang Grottoes.

Cave 18 (Cave of Three Standing Buddhas) 460-470 CE Cave 18, Cave 19 and Cave 20 make a group. Cave 19 is at the center and was the earliest among the group. Cave 18 is carefully designed in layout and arrangement. Its central Buddha on the north wall is 15.5 meters high, wearing a high ushnisha, round cheeks and high nose bridge, and a kasaya with Thousand-Buddha pattern. Flanking on both side are attendant Buddhas, Bodhisattvas and ten great disciples. The attendant Buddha on the left has a canopy hanging over the head. The attendant Bodhisattva on the left wears a flowery crown. All of the five great disciples on the right show characteristics of people from the Western Regions, some standing quietly with a vase, some holding flowers and smiling, some listening with eyes closed, and some appearing enlightened, or in deep joy. The uncanny craftsmanship shown here is simply amazing.

Cave 19 (Cave of Ratnasambhava Buddha) 460-470 CE The central Buddha seated in lotus position is 16.8 meters in height. It is the second largest Buddha in the Yungang Grottoes. The earlobes of Buddha are elongated, and the jaw partly collapsed. Buddha's right hand is raised, supported by a small pillar under the elbow. The clothing pattern is simple and lively, so thin that it shows the body curves clearly. Buddha's kasaya is decorated with folded belt patterns. The depiction of a scene from the Nidana tale "Vyakarana of Rahula" is the earliest narrative art created in the Yungang Grottoes. Two chambers on the east and west sides of the cave's front wall were dug out, each housing a throne-sitting Buddha statue inside. This design of side chambers to accommodate the Tryadhva-Buddha motif is a new innovation in terms of layout design during North Wei dynasty. The front wall used to have an entrance archway and an upper window, and probably collapsed about the same time as the front wall of Cave 20.

Cave 20 (Cave of White Buddha) 460-470 CE The front wall and ceiling of Cave 20 collapsed early on, and a wooden eaves was built during Liao dynasty, which was later destroyed by war, leaving the statues in the open since, as we see them today. The central Buddha is 13.7 meters in height, with a high ushnisha, wide forehead, ample cheeks, long eyes, high nose and a conspicuous mustache, seated in lotus position, holding a meditation mudra with both hands, and wearing a thick kasaya with right shoulder laid bare and protruding patterns, all of which show a Gandharan influence. The tall and strong physique of Buddha with its majestic expression seems to symbolize the strength of the Xianbei nomadic people. It is a representative work of art from the Yungang Grottoes, and also illustrates the achievement of early Chinese Buddhist art. An attendant Buddha and Bodhisattva used to be flanking both sides, unfortunately the west side ones are lost.

Cave 21-45 (West End Caves) 494-525 CE After Emperor Xiaowen relocated the capital city to Luoyang in 494 CE, the large-scale imperial projects at Yungang Grottoes were halted, then soon continued by local worshippers until the years of Zhengguang Reign of Emperor Xiaoming. Most of the caves from this period were medium- and small-sized ones, with various types of layout and styles. Three-niches-on-four-walls and layered-niches-on-three-walls were the popular types. The popular Buddhist images included Tryadhva-Buddha, Sakyamuni & Maitreya Buddha, Sakyamuni & Prabhuta-ratna Buddha and Vimalakirti with Manjushri Bodhisattva, etc. The statues were always in the ample-gown-and-loose-girdle style, with elegantly slim figure; Bodhisattvas usually wrapped in silk scarves, with thin necks and round shoulders; Apsaras were also of slim figures and wearing long skirts. Tympanum and trabeation were decorated with even more complicated motifs. During this period, Chinese Buddhist arts had been fully sinicized and secularized, and the birth of the Longmen Grottoes was right around the corner.

18
17
16
15
14
13
12
11
10

11
10
9
8
7

← 自右向左阅读

027
第 3 窟 灵岩寺洞

003
第 1 窟 石鼓洞

015
第 2 窟 寒泉洞

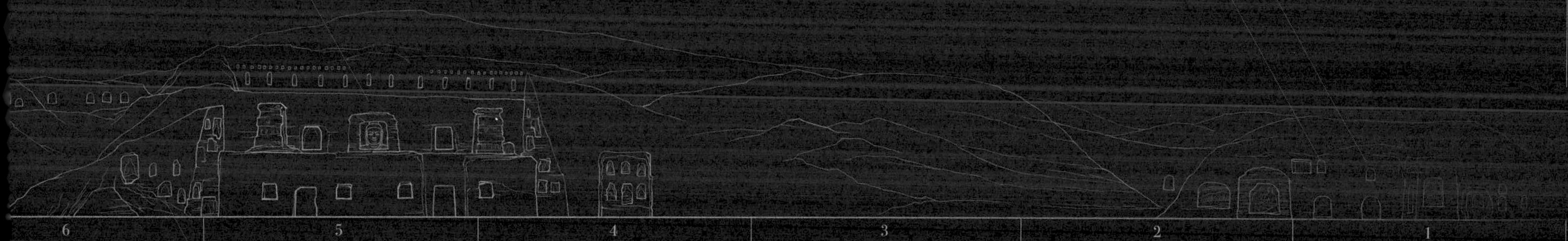

第 4 窟（晚期）

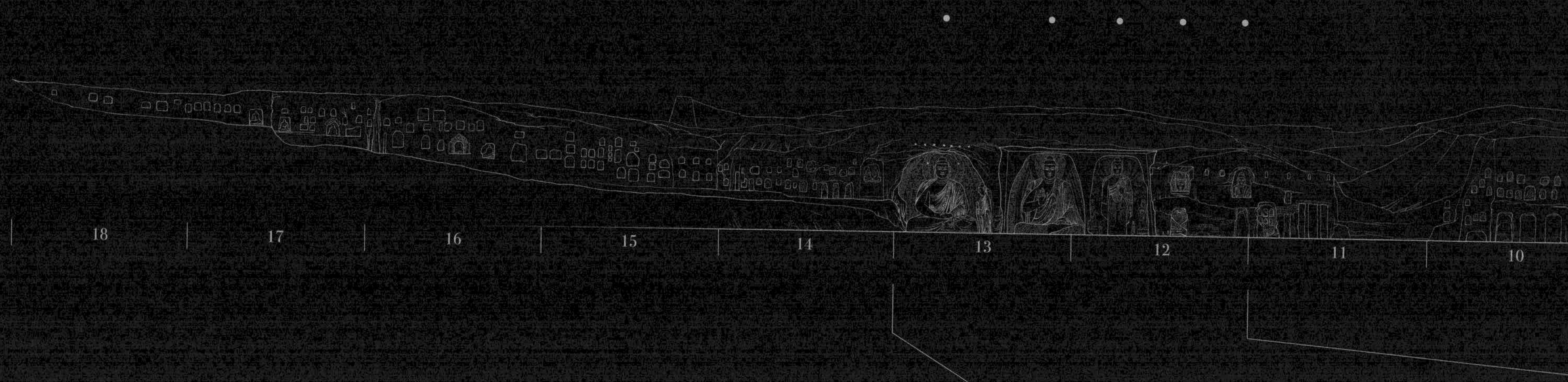

577

第 20 窟 白佛爷洞

← 自右向左阅读

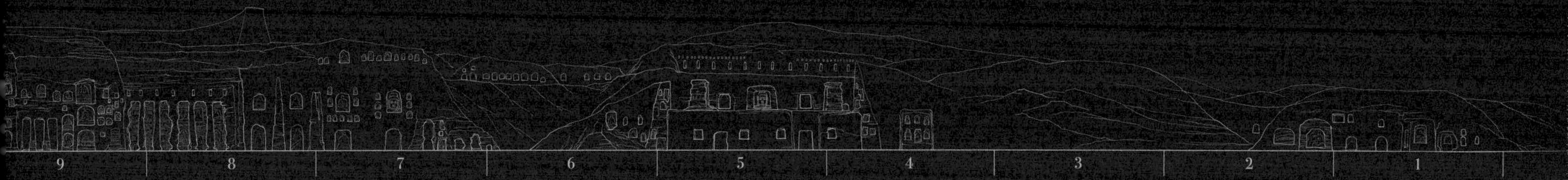
9
8
7
6
5
4
3
2
1

493
第 18 窟 立三佛洞
437
第 17 窟 弥勒三尊洞
371
第 16 窟 立佛洞
12
535
第 19 窟 宝生佛洞

18
17
16
15
14
13
12
11
10
第 44 窟
第 42 窟
第 40 窟
第 38 窟
第 36 窟
第 35 窟
第 34 窟
18
17
16
第 45 窟
第 43 窟
第 41 窟
第 39 窟
第 37 窟

← 自右向左阅读

第 21 窟—第 45 窟，14-18

云冈石窟申报世界
文化遗产成功碑

大佛寺
第1~6窟
CAVES NO

第1~6窟
CAVES NO.1~6

1500 年前

他们耗时 64 年用信仰与钎斧开凿了云冈石窟

1500 年后

他们历时 10 年用大画幅胶片记录了云冈石窟

1500 years ago

They spent 64 years digging the Yungang Grottoes with faith and ch

1500 years later

They spent 10 years documenting the Yungang Grottoes on large fo

本书摄影

赵富义　宫品仁

Photographiers

Zhao Fuyi　Gong Pinren

第一幅

	a	b	c	d
1				
2				
3				
4				

004 – 009

第二幅

	a	b
1		
2		
3		
4		
5		
6		

010 – 013

第1窟
（石鼓洞）
公元471-494年

第
一
幅

第1窟　西壁　West Wall

第1窟　第一幅，c-d，1-2

第 1 窟　第一幅，d，3-4

第 1 窟　第一幅，a-d，2-3

第1窟
（石鼓洞）
公元471-494年

第二幅

第 1 窟　东壁睒子本生故事图　Jataka Tale of Syama, East Wall

第 1 窟　第二幅，a，1-3

第 1 窟　第二幅，b，1-3

第一幅

016 – 021

第二幅

022 – 025

第 2 窟
（寒泉洞）
公元 471-494 年

第一幅

第 2 窟　中心柱　Central Pillar

第2窟　第一幅，b-d，1-3

第 2 窟　第一幅，d-e，2-3

第2窟　第一幅，a-e，2-4

第 2 窟
（寒泉洞）
公元 471-494 年

第
二
幅

第 2 窟　东壁盝形龛　Truncated-Tent Shaped Niche, East Wall

第 2 窟　第二幅，a-b，1-3

第一幅

030 – 031

第二幅

032–035

第三幅

036 – 039

第四幅

040 – 041

第五幅

042 – 045

第六幅

046 – 049

第七幅

050 – 053

第3窟
（灵岩寺洞）
公元471-494年

第
一
幅

第 3 窟　后室内景　Interior, Back Chamber

第 3 窟
（灵岩寺洞）
公元 471-494 年

第二幅

第 3 窟　后室主像　Central Statue, Back Chamber

第 3 窟　第二幅，a-c，4-6

第3窟　第二幅，c-f，1-3

第3窟
（灵岩寺洞）
公元471-494年

第
三
幅

第 3 窟　后室主像西方三圣　Amitabha Triad, Back Chamber

第 3 窟　第三幅，b-e，1-2

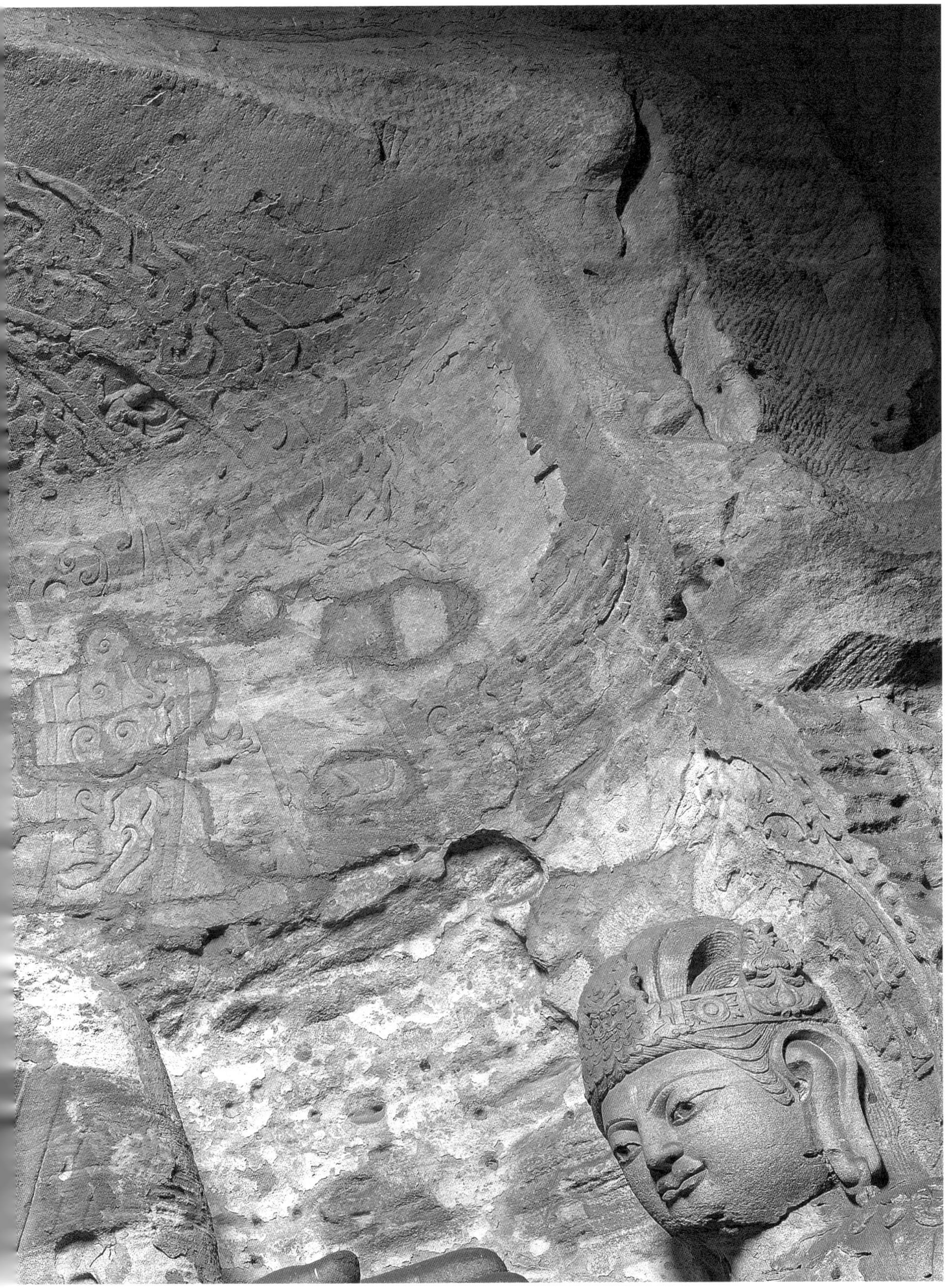

第3窟
（灵岩寺洞）
公元471-494年

第
四
幅

第 3 窟　左胁侍菩萨　Left Side Attendant Bodhisattva

第 3 窟
（灵岩寺洞）
公元 471-494 年

第
五
幅

第 3 窟　后室左胁侍菩萨　Left Side Attendant Bodhisattva, Back Chamber

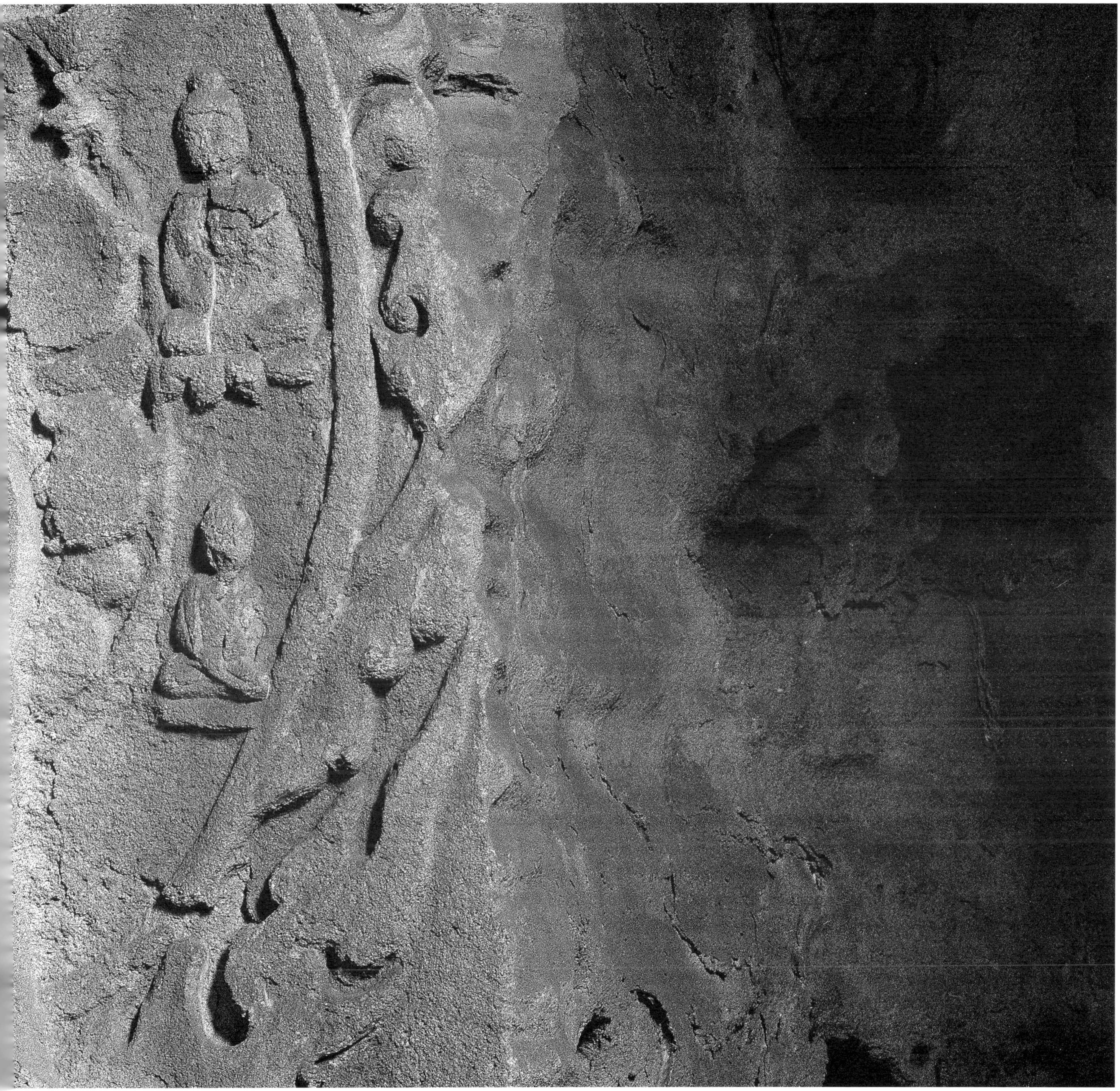

第 3 窟　第五幅，c-f，4-6

第 3 窟

（灵岩寺洞）

公元 471-494 年

第六幅

第 3 窟　右胁侍菩萨　Right Side Attendant Bodhisattva

第 3 窟　第六幅，b-e，1-2

第3窟　第六幅，a-e，4-5

第3窟
（灵岩寺洞）
公元471-494年

第
七
幅

第 3 窟　窟外平台上东侧圆雕塔　Square Pagoda, East Side of Terrace Outside Cave 3

第 3 窟　第七幅，b-d，1-2

第3窟　第七幅，b-d，3-4

a b c d

第一幅

1 2 3 4 5 6

058 – 059

a b c

第二幅

1 2 3 4

060 – 063

064

第三幅

065-067

第四幅

068 – 069

第五幅

第六幅

070 – 073

第七幅

074 – 077

第 5 窟
（大佛洞）
公元 471-494 年

第
一
幅

第 5 窟　北壁主佛　Central Statue, North Wall

第5窟
（大佛洞）
公元471-494年

第二幅

第 5 窟　窟内西半部　West Side of Interior

第5窟　第二幅，a，2-3

第 5 窟　第三幅，窟门西壁树下二佛　Seated Buddhas under Tree, West Wall of Entrance Gateway

第 5 窟　第四幅，窟门东壁树下二佛　Seated Buddhas under Tree, East Wall of Entrance Gateway

第 5 窟　第四幅，窟门东壁树下二佛

第 5 窟　第四幅，窟门东壁树下二佛

第 5 窟
（大佛洞）
公元 471-494 年

第
五
幅

第5窟　窟门东壁金刚力士　Vajra-Warrior, East Wall of Entrance Gateway

第5窟
（大佛洞）
公元471-494年

第
六
幅

第 5 窟附属窟　北壁佛像　Buddha Statue, North Wall

第 5 窟附属窟　第六幅，a-e，2-3

第 5 窟
（大佛洞）
公元 471-494 年

第七幅

第 5 窟　明窗西壁千佛　Thousand-Buddha Motif, West Wall of Upper Window

第5窟　第七幅，b-d，2-5

第一幅

a b c d e

1 2 3 4 5

082–085

第二幅

a b c d e

1 2 3 4 5

086 – 089

第三幅

090 – 091

第四幅

092

第五幅

093

第六幅

094 – 095

096

第七幅

097

第八幅

098

第九幅

099

第十幅

100 – 101

第十一幅

102 – 103

第十二幅

104 – 105

第十三幅

106

第十四幅

107

第十五幅

108

第十六幅

109

第十七幅

第十八幅

110 – 113

第十九幅

114 – 117

第6窟

（释迦佛洞）

公元471-494年

第一幅

第 6 窟　中心塔柱下层东面交脚菩萨　Cross-ankled Bodhisattva, East Side of Lower Level of Central Pillar

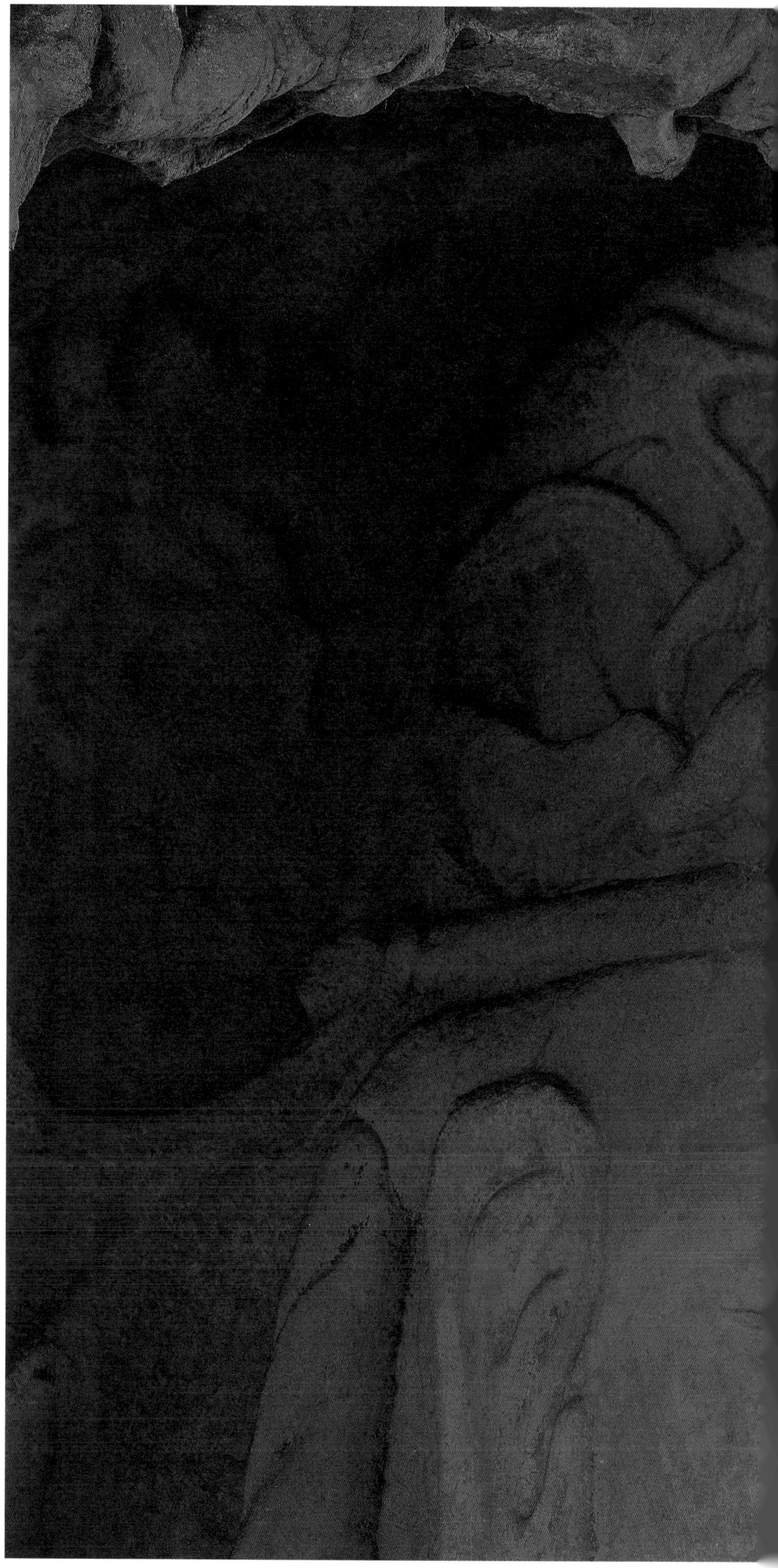

第6窟　第一幅，b-e，1-2

第6窟
（释迦佛洞）
公元471-494年

第二幅

第 6 窟　中心塔柱南面下层供养天众　Offering Devas, South Side of Lower Level of Central Pillar

第 6 窟　第二幅，a-e，1-2

第6窟
（释迦佛洞）
公元471-494年

第
三
幅

 第 6 窟　中心塔柱南面下层供养天众　Offering Devas, South Side of Lower Level of Central Pillar

第 6 窟　第四幅，中心塔柱东面下层护法夜叉　Dharmapala Yaksa, East Side of Lower Level of Central Pillar

第 6 窟　第五幅，中心塔柱西面下层护法夜叉　Dharmapala Yaksa, West Side of Lower Level of Central Pillar

第 6 窟
（释迦佛洞）
公元 471-494 年

第
六
幅

第 6 窟　中心塔柱东面下层护法像　Dharmapala, East Side of Lower Level of Central Pillar

第 6 窟　第七幅，中心塔柱南面下层金翅鸟　Garuda, South Side of Lower Level of Central Pillar

第 6 窟　第八幅，中心塔柱南面下层金翅鸟　Garuda, South Side of Lower Level of Central Pillar

第 6 窟　第九幅，中心塔柱下层南面礼贺母胎佛传图　Scene of "Congratulating Mayadevi" from Biographical Tales of Buddha, South Side of Lower Level of Central Pillar

第 6 窟　第十幅，中心塔柱下层北面阿私陀占相佛传图　Scene of "Asita's Divination" from Biographical Tales of Buddha, North Side of Lower Level of Central Pillar

第6窟
（释迦佛洞）
公元471-494年

第十一幅

第 6 窟　中心塔柱西面下层父子回城佛传图　Scene of “Returning with Father”, West Side of Central Pillar of Central Pillar

第 6 窟　第十二幅，中心塔柱西面腋下诞生佛传图　Scene of Birth from Biographical Tales of Buddha, West Side of Central Pillar

第 6 窟
（释迦佛洞）
公元 471-494 年

第十三幅

第 6 窟　东壁佛像　Buddha, East Wall

第 6 窟　第十四幅，东壁太子较艺佛传图　Scene of "Archery Contest" from Biographical Tales of Buddha, East Wall

第 6 窟　第十五幅，东壁宫中娱乐佛传图　Scene of “Mundane Joys” from Biographical Tales of Buddha, East Wall

第 6 窟　第十六幅，东壁父子对话佛传图　Scene of "Conversation between Father and Son" from Biographical Tales of Buddha, East Wall

第 6 窟　第十七幅，东壁出门遇老人佛传图　Scene of "Seeing an Old Man" from Biographical Tales of Buddha, East Wall

第 6 窟
（释迦佛洞）
公元 471-494 年

第
十
八
幅

第 6 窟　南壁维摩诘经故事图　Scene from *Vimalakirti Sutra*, South Wall

3　　第6窟　第十八幅，f-h，3

第 6 窟
（释迦佛洞）
公元 471-494 年

第十九幅

第 6 窟　南壁西侧龛供养天众　Offering Devas, West Side Niche of South Wall

第 6 窟　第十九幅，a-c，1-3

第 6 窟　第十九幅，b-d，3-6

第一幅

122 – 125

第二幅

126–130

第三幅

131

第四幅

132 – 133

第五幅

134 – 137

第六幅

138 – 141

第七幅

142

第八幅

143

第九幅

146 – 147

第十幅

148 – 149

第十一幅

150 – 153

第7窟
（西来第一佛洞）
公元471-494年

第一幅

第 7 窟　后室北壁上层主像　Statues of Upper Portion, North Wall of Back Chamber

第7窟　第一幅，c-f，1-4

第7窟　第一幅，g-h，1-3

第7窟
（西来第一佛洞）
公元471-494年

第
二
幅

第 7 窟　后室西壁　West Wall, Back Chamber

第 7 窟　第二幅，a-f，1-2

第 7 窟　第三幅，后室西壁南侧盝形龛　Truncated-Tent Shaped Niche, South Side of West Wall of Back Chamber

第7窟
（西来第一佛洞）
公元471-494年

第
四
幅

第 7 窟　后室西壁重层塔柱　Multi-Storied Pagoda in Relief, West Wall of Back Chamber

第 7 窟

（西来第一佛洞）

公元 471-494 年

第五幅

第 7 窟　后室南壁文殊菩萨　Manjushri Bodhisattva, South Wall of Back Chamber

第7窟　第五幅，a，2-3

第7窟　第五幅，c-d，2-3

第 7 窟
（西来第一佛洞）
公元 471-494 年

第六幅

第 7 窟　窟门西侧方形重层塔柱　Multi-Storied Square Pagoda, West Side of Entrance Gateway

第 7 窟　第六幅，a-b，2-6

第7窟　第六幅，c-d，1-3

第 7 窟　第七幅，窟门西壁　West Wall, Entrance Gateway

第 7 窟　第八幅，窟门东壁　East Wall, Entrance Gateway

第 7 窟　第七幅，窟门西壁细节　Details of the West Wall of the Entrance Gateway

第 7 窟　第八幅，窟门东壁细节　Details of the East Wall of the Entrance Gateway

第 7 窟
（西来第一佛洞）
公元 471-494 年

第九幅

第 7 窟　窟门西壁化生童子　Kumara Upa-paduka, West Wall of Entrance Gateway

第 7 窟
（西来第一佛洞）
公元 471-494 年

第
十
幅

49　第 7 窟　后室南壁窟门与明窗之间供养天——“云冈六美人”　Offering Devas, between Upper Window and Entrance Gateway of South Wall of Back Chamber

第 7 窟
（佛籁洞）
公元 471-494 年

第十一幅

第 7 窟　后室窟顶平棊藻井　Coffered Ceiling, Back Chamber

第7窟　第十一幅，c-g，3-6

156-157

第一幅

162-163

第三幅

第四幅

164 – 167

第二幅

158 – 161

168 – 169

第五幅

第 8 窟

（佛籁洞）

公元 471-494 年

第一幅

第 8 窟　窟门西壁鸠摩罗天　Kumara, West Side of Entrance Gateway

第8窟
（佛籁洞）
公元471-494年

第
二
幅

第 8 窟　窟门东壁摩醯首罗天　Maheshvara, East Side of Entrance Gateway

第 8 窟　第二幅，a-b，4-5

第 8 窟　第二幅，b-c，3-4

第 8 窟
（佛籁洞）
公元 471-494 年

第
三
幅

第 8 窟　后室东壁降魔成道故事图右侧魔众　Armies of Demons, Right Portion of Sculptural Relief "Assault on Buddha by Mara", East Wall of Back Chamber

第 8 窟
（佛籁洞）
公元 471-494 年

第
四
幅

第 8 窟　后室南壁窟门　Entrance, South Wall of Back Chamber

第 8 窟　第四幅，c-j，1

第8窟
（佛籁洞）
公元471-494年

第
五
幅

第 8 窟　后室窟门西侧俗众　Laymen worshippers, West Side of Entrance Gateway, Back Chamber

第一幅

174 – 177

第二幅

178 – 179

第三幅

180–183

184

第四幅

185

第五幅

186 – 187

第六幅

第七幅

188 – 191

第八幅

192–197

第九幅

198–201

第十幅

202 – 205

第十一幅

206 – 209

第十二幅

210　211

第9窟
（阿閦佛洞）
公元471-494年

第
一
幅

第 9 窟　外壁全景　Full Front View

77 第9窟 第一幅，外壁明窗

第9窟
（阿閦佛洞）
公元471-494年

第二幅

第 9 窟　前室南壁列柱　Columns, South Wall of Antechamber

第9窟
（阿閦佛洞）
公元471-494年

第
三
幅

1 第 9 窟 前室北壁 North Wall of Antechamber

第 9 窟　第三幅，b-e，1-3

第 9 窟　第四幅，前室北壁窟门上方装饰　Decorative Motifs, Top of Entrance Gateway, North Wall of Antechamber

第 9 窟　第五幅，前室北壁窟门上方飞天局部　Details of Apsaras, Top of Entrance Gateway, North Wall of Antechamber

第 9 窟
（阿閦佛洞）
公元 471-494 年

第
六
幅

第 9 窟　北壁窟门顶部飞天　Apsaras, Inside Entrance Gateway, North Wall of Antechamber

第 9 窟
（阿閦佛洞）
公元 471-494 年

第
七
幅

第 9 窟　前室北壁下层西龛　West Niche, Lower Portion of North Wall of Antechamber

第9窟　第七幅，a，3

第 9 窟　第七幅，b-d，4-5

第9窟
(阿閦佛洞)
公元471-494年

第
八
幅

第 9 窟　前室西壁上半部　Upper portion, West Wall of Antechamber

第9窟　第八幅，c-d，1-2

第 9 窟　第八幅，e-f，2-3

第9窟　第八幅，d-e，5-6

第9窟
（阿閦佛洞）
公元471-494年

第
九
幅

第 9 窟　前室东壁下层北侧佛龛　North Niche, Lower Portion of East Wall of Antechamber

第9窟　第九幅，b-f，3

第 9 窟　第九幅，c-j，1

第9窟
（阿閦佛洞）
公元471-494年

第
十
幅

第 9 窟　后室顶部　Ceiling of Back Chamber

第9窟　第十幅，b-f，2-3

第9窟
（阿閦佛洞）
公元471-494年

第十一幅

第 9 窟　后室南壁　South Wall of Back Chamber

第 9 窟　第十一幅，f-h，1-2

第9窟　第十一幅，a-c，1-2

第 9 窟　第十二幅，后室南壁窟门上方　Top of Entrance Gateway, South Wall of Back Chamber

第一幅

214 – 217

第二幅

218 – 221

222 – 223

第三幅

第四幅

224 – 227

228 – 229

第五幅

230

第六幅

231

第七幅

第10窟
（毗卢佛洞）
公元471-494年

第一幅

第 10 窟 前室北壁明窗 Upper Window, North Wall of Antechamber

第10窟　第一幅，f-g，1-2

第 10 窟
（毗卢佛洞）
公元 471-494 年

第
二
幅

第 10 窟　前室北壁窟门上方须弥山　Mount Sumeru, Top of Entrance Gateway, North Wall of Antechamber

第10窟　第二幅，a-c，3-5

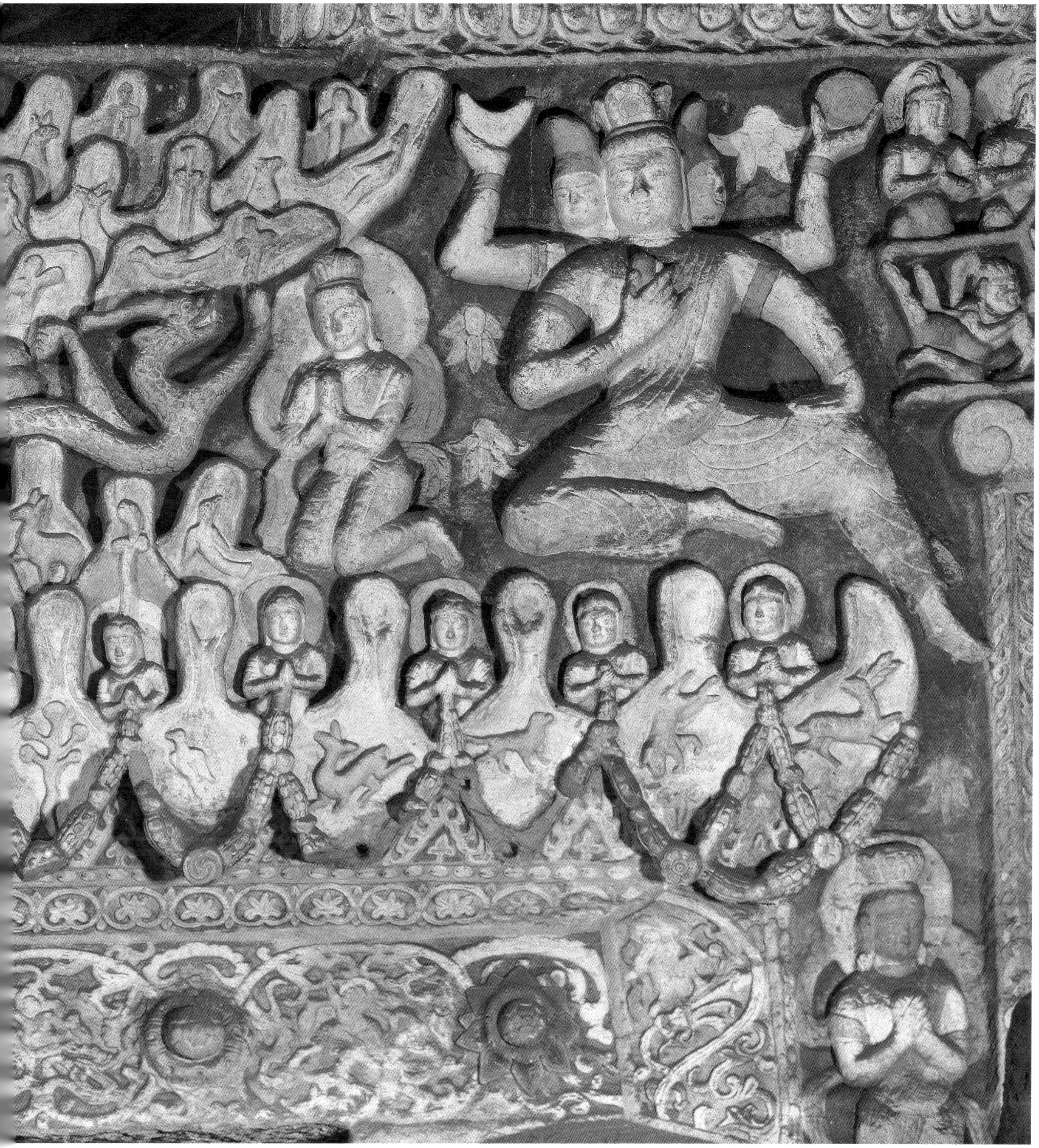

第10窟
（毗卢佛洞）
公元471-494年

第三幅

第 10 窟　窟门顶部托炉飞天　Apsara Holding an Incense-Burner, Top of Entrance Gateway

第10窟
（毗卢佛洞）
公元471-494年

第
四
幅

第 10 窟　后室南壁窟门　Entrance Gateway, South Wall of Back Chamber

第 10 窟　第四幅，a-c，2-4

第 10 窟　第五幅，后室南壁窟门上方　Top of Entrance Gateway, South Wall of Back Chamber

第 10 窟　第六幅，后室南壁西侧因缘故事图　Scene of Nidana Tales, West Side of South Wall of Back Chamber

第 10 窟　第七幅，后室南壁西侧降魔成道故事图　Scene of "Assault on Buddha by Mara", West side of South Wall of Back Chamber

第一幅

234 – 237

第二幅

238 – 241

第三幅

242 – 243

第四幅

244 – 247

第五幅

248 – 249

第六幅

250 – 251

第 11 窟
（接引佛洞）
公元 471-494 年

第
一
幅

第 11 窟　西壁七立佛　Seven Standing Buddhas, West Wall

第 11 窟　第一幅，a-c，1

第 11 窟
（接引佛洞）
公元 471-494 年

第二幅

第 11 窟　西壁七立佛之一　Detail A of Seven Standing Buddhas, West Wall

第 11 窟　第二幅，b-e，2 3

第11窟
（接引佛洞）
公元471-494年

第三幅

第 11 窟　西壁七立佛之二　Detail B of Seven Standing Buddhas, West Wall

第 11 窟

（接引佛洞）

公元 471-494 年

第四幅

第 11 窟　西壁盝形龛交脚菩萨　Cross-Ankled Bodhisattva, Truncated-Tent Shaped Niche of West Wall

第 11 窟　第四幅，a-b，1-2

第 11 窟　第四幅，a-b，3-5

第 11 窟
(接引佛洞)
公元 471-494 年

第五幅

第 11 窟　南壁交脚菩萨　Cross-Ankled Bodhisattva, South Wall

第11窟
（接引佛洞）
公元471-494年

第
六
幅

第 11 窟　南壁交脚菩萨头像　Head of Cross-Ankled Bodhisattva, South Wall

第一幅

256 – 259

第二幅

260 – 261

第三幅

262 – 265

第四幅

266 – 269

第五幅

270

第六幅

271

第七幅

272

第八幅

273

第九幅

274－275

第十幅

276

第十一幅

277

第十二幅

278

第十三幅

279

第十四幅

280－281

第十五幅

282－283

a	b	c	d	e	f	g	h

1
2
3
4
5

第十六幅

284 – 287

第十七幅

288 – 289

第 12 窟
（离垢地菩萨洞）
公元 471-494 年

第
一
幅

第 12 窟　前室北壁　North Wall, Antechamber

第 12 窟　第一幅，a-b，2

第12窟
(离垢地菩萨洞)
公元471-494年

第
二
幅

第 12 窟　窟门顶部交龙　Intertwined-Dragon Motif, Top of Entrance Gateway

第12窟
（离垢地菩萨洞）
公元471-494年

第
三
幅

第 12 窟　前室东壁上层　Upper Portion, East Wall of Antechamber

第 12 窟　第三幅，b-c，1-2

第12窟
（离垢地菩萨洞）
公元471-494年

第
四
幅

第 12 窟　前室西壁上层交脚佛　Cross-Ankled Buddha, Upper Portion of West Wall of Antechamber

第 12 窟　第四幅，a-d，1-2

第 12 窟　第五幅，前室东壁上层龛右胁思惟菩萨　Right Side Pensive Bodhisattva, Upper Portion Niche of East Wall of Antechamber

第 12 窟　第六幅，前室东壁上层龛左胁思惟菩萨　Left Side Pensive Bodhisattva, Upper Portion Niche of East Wall of Antechamber

第 12 窟　第七幅，前室西壁飞天　Apsara, West Wall of Antechamber

第 12 窟　第八幅，前室西壁降伏火龙故事图局部　Detail of "Buddha Subduing Fire-Dragon" Scene, West Wall of Antechamber

第 12 窟　第九幅，前室西部上端　Upper Portion, West Side of Antechamber

第 12 窟　第十幅，前室窟顶南侧弹指伎　Finger-Snapping Celestial Musician, South Side of Antechamber Ceiling

第 12 窟　第十一幅，前室窟顶东侧琵琶伎　Celestial Musician Playing Pipa, East Side of Antechamber Ceiling

第 12 窟　第十二幅，前室窟顶东南侧筚篥伎　Celestial Musician Playing Bili, South-East Side of Antechamber Ceiling

第 12 窟　第十三幅，前室窟顶南侧腰鼓伎　Celestial Musician Playing Waist Drum, South Side of Antechamber Ceiling

第12窟
（离垢地菩萨洞）
公元471-494年

第十四幅

第 12 窟　前室窟顶　Antechamber Ceiling

第12窟
（离垢地菩萨洞）
公元471-494年

第
十
五
幅

第 12 窟　后室窟顶　Back Chamber Ceiling

第 12 窟

（离垢地菩萨洞）

公元 471-494 年

第十六幅

第 12 窟　后室南壁上层　Upper Portion, South Wall of Back Chamber

第 12 窟　第十六幅，b-g，4-5

第 12 窟
（离垢地菩萨洞）
公元 471-494 年

第十七幅

第 12 窟　后室南壁东龛胡商　Sogdian Merchants, East Niche of South Wall of Back Chamber

a b c d e

第一幅

1 2 3 4 5

294 – 297

298 – 299

第二幅

a b c d e f g h i

第三幅

1 2 3 4 5 6 7 8

300 – 303

304 – 305

第四幅

306 – 307

第五幅

308 – 309

第六幅

310

第七幅

311

第八幅

第九幅

312 – 315

316

第十幅

317

第十一幅

第 13 窟
（文殊菩萨洞）
公元 471-494 年

第一幅

第 13 窟　北壁主像交脚菩萨　Cross-Ankled Bodhisattva, Central Statue of North Wall

第 13 窟　第一幅，b-e，2-3

第13窟

（文殊菩萨洞）

公元471-494年

第

二

幅

第 13 窟　第二幅，北壁主像托臂力士　Guardian Lifting Bodhisattva's Forearm, Detail of Central Statue of North Wall

第 13 窟
（文殊菩萨洞）
公元 471-494 年

第
三
幅

第 13 窟　东壁盝形龛交脚菩萨　Cross-Ankled Bodhisattva, Truncated-Tent Shaped Niche of East Wall

第 13 窟　第三幅，b-e，2-3

第 13 窟　第三幅，d-h，4-6

第13窟
（文殊菩萨洞）
公元471-494年

第
四
幅

第 13 窟　东壁下层供养天　Offering Deva, Lower Portion of East Wall

第13窟
（文殊菩萨洞）
公元471-494年

第
五
幅

第 13 窟　南壁　South Wall

第 13 窟　第六幅，南壁七佛局部　Detail A of Seven Buddhas, South Wall

第 13 窟　第七幅，南壁七佛之一　Detail B of Seven Buddhas, South Wall

第 13 窟　第八幅，南壁七佛之二　Detail C of Seven Buddhas, South Wall

第13窟
（文殊菩萨洞）
公元471-494年

第
九
幅

第 13 窟　南壁东半部　East Side of South Wall

第 13 窟　第九幅，c，2

第 13 窟　第九幅，d，4

第 13 窟　第十幅，南壁飞天　Apsara, South Wall

第 13 窟　第十一幅，南壁伎乐飞天　Celestial Musician, South Wall

第一幅

322 – 323

第二幅

324–331

第三幅

332 – 337

第四幅

338 – 339

第五幅

340 – 341

第六幅

342

第七幅

343

第14窟
公元494-525年

第一幅

第14窟　内景　Interior

第 14 窟
公元 494-525 年

第二幅

第 14 窟　前室西壁　West Wall, Antechamber

27

第14窟　第二幅，b-c，1-2

第14窟　第二幅，b-d，3

第14窟　第二幅，c-d，6

第14窟
公元494-525年

第三幅

第 14 窟　前室西壁龛像　Niche with Statues, West Wall of Antechamber

第 14 窟　第三幅，b-c，1-2

第 14 窟　第三幅，a-b，1-5

第14窟　第三幅，b-d，5-8

第14窟
公元494-525年

第四幅

第 14 窟　东廊柱　East Corridor Column

第 14 窟
公元 494-525 年

第五幅

第 14 窟　内廊柱　Interior Corridor Column

第 14 窟　第六幅，后室东壁上层　Upper Portion, East Wall of Back Chamber

第 14 窟　第七幅，前室南壁帷幔上端龛像　Niches above Hanging Curtain Motif, South Wall of Antechamber

第一幅

348 – 351

352 – 353

第二幅

第三幅

354 – 357

358 – 359

第四幅

360 – 361

第五幅

362 – 363

第六幅

364

第七幅

365

第八幅

366

第九幅

367

第十幅

368

第十一幅

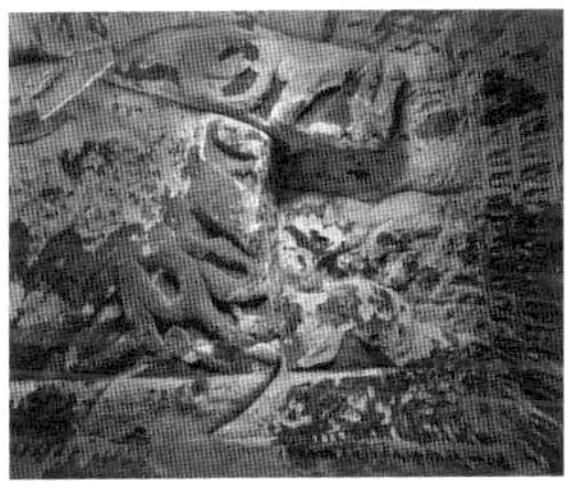

369

第十二幅

第15窟
（万佛洞）
公元494-525年

第
一
幅

第15窟　西壁　West Wall

第 15 窟　第一幅，a-c，4-5

第 15 窟
（万佛洞）
公元 494-525 年

第
二
幅

第 15 窟　西壁千佛　Thousan-Buddha Motif, West Wall

第15窟
（万佛洞）
公元494-525年

第
三
幅

第 15 窟　西壁坐佛龛　Niche with Seated Buddha, West Wall

第 15 窟　第三幅，a-c，4-7

第15窟　第三幅，d-e，3-4

第 15 窟
（万佛洞）
公元 494-525 年

第
四
幅

第 15 窟　西壁上部千佛龛　Thousand-Buddha Niche, Upper Portion of West Wall

第 15 窟
（万佛洞）
公元 494-525 年

第
五
幅

第 15 窟　东壁下层坐佛龛　Seated Buddha Niche, Lower Portion of East Wall

第15窟

（万佛洞）

公元494-525年

第

六

幅

第 15 窟　南壁　South Wall

第 15 窟　第七幅，窟顶东南角　South-East Corner, Cave Ceiling

第 15 窟　第八幅，窟顶交龙　Intertwined-Dragon Motif, Cave Ceiling

第 15 窟　第九幅，窟顶东北角　North-East Corner, Cave Ceiling

第 15 窟　第十幅，窟顶西北角　North-West Corner, Cave Ceiling

第 15 窟　第十一幅，窟顶东南角　South-East Corner, Cave Ceiling

第 15 窟　第十二幅，窟顶南侧交龙　Intertwined-Dragon Motif, South Side of Cave Ceiling

第一幅

374 – 375

第二幅

376 – 377

第三幅

378 – 379

第四幅

380 – 383

第五幅

384－385

第六幅

386－387

第七幅

388－389

第八幅

390－393

第九幅

394－395

第十幅

396－397

第十一幅

398－399

第十二幅

400－401

第十三幅

402

第十四幅

403

第十五幅

404－405

第十六幅

406

第十七幅

407

第十八幅

408 – 411

第十九幅

412 – 413

第二十幅

414 – 415

第二十一幅

416 – 421

第二十二幅

422 – 427

第二十三幅

428 – 429

第二十四幅

430 – 431

第二十五幅

432 – 433

第二十六幅

434 – 435

第16窟
（立佛洞）
公元460-470年

第
一
幅

第 16 窟　北壁主佛　Central Buddha, North Wall

第16窟
（立佛洞）
公元460-470年

第
二
幅

第 16 窟　北壁主佛　Central Buddha, North Wall

第 16 窟　第三幅，北壁佛像特写　Detail of Central Buddha, North Wall

第 16 窟
（立佛洞）
公元 460-470 年

第
四
幅

第 16 窟　北壁主佛手印特写　Detail of Central Buddha's Mudras, North Wall

第 16 窟　第四幅，a-c，1-2

第16窟　第四幅，d-f，1-3

第16窟
（立佛洞）
公元460-470年

第
五
幅

第16窟　东壁佛龛胁侍菩萨头部特写　Detail of Head, Attendant Bodhisattva of East Wall Niche

第16窟
（立佛洞）
公元460-470年

第六幅

第 16 窟　东壁佛龛佛像特写　Detail of Buddha, East Wall Niche

第 16 窟
（立佛洞）
公元 460-470 年

第
七
幅

第 16 窟　东壁佛龛右侧弟子　Right Side Disciple, East Wall Niche

第16窟
（立佛洞）
公元460-470年

第
八
幅

第 16 窟　东壁佛龛左侧弟子　Left Side Disciple, East Wall Niche

第 16 窟　第八幅，b-e，1-2

第16窟　第八幅，b-d，3-5

第 16 窟
（立佛洞）
公元 460-470 年

第
九
幅

第 16 窟　南壁西侧佛龛　West Niche of South Wall

第 16 窟　第十幅，南壁龛外右上隅伎乐天　Celestial Musicians, Upper Right Corner Outside South Wall Niche

第 16 窟　第十一幅，南壁龛外左上隅伎乐天　Celestial Musicians, Upper Left Corner Outside South Wall Niche

第16窟
（立佛洞）
公元460-470年

第十二幅

第 16 窟　南壁西侧佛龛内右胁侍菩萨　Right Side Attendant Bodhisattva, West Niche of South Wall

第 16 窟　第十三幅，南壁西侧佛龛外供养天　Offering Deva Outside West Niche of South Wall

第 16 窟　第十四幅，南壁西侧佛龛左侧拱尾反首龙　Dragon with Back-Turning Head and Arching Tail, Left Side of West Niche of South Wall

第16窟
（立佛洞）
公元460-470年

第
十
五
幅

第 16 窟　南壁东侧交脚菩萨龛　Cross-Ankled Bodhisattva Niche, East Side of South Wall

第 16 窟　第十六幅，南壁东侧右上隅供养天　Offering Deva, Upper Right Corner of East Side of South Wall

第 16 窟　第十七幅，南壁东侧内左胁侍半跏思惟菩萨　Half-Lotus-Seated Pensive Bodhisattva, Left Side of East Niche of South Wall

第16窟
（立佛洞）
公元460-470年

第
十
八
幅

第 16 窟　南壁东侧龛菩萨头像　Head of Bodhisattva, East Niche of South Wall

第16窟　第十八幅，a-b，1-2

第 16 窟　第十九幅，南壁东侧佛龛龛楣外右侧伎乐天　Celestial Musicians, Right Corner Outside East Niche of South Wall

第 16 窟　第二十幅，南壁东侧佛龛龛楣左侧伎乐天　Celestial Musicians, Left Corner Outside East Niche of South Wall

第 16 窟
（立佛洞）
公元 460-470 年

第二十一幅

第 16 窟　明窗西壁龛像　Niche with Statues, West Wall of Upper Window

第 16 窟　第二十一幅，b-e，1

第16窟　第二十一幅，c-d，3

第 16 窟
（立佛洞）
公元 460-470 年

第二十二幅

第 16 窟　明窗东壁龛像　Niche with Statues, East Wall of Upper Window

第 16 窟　第二十二幅，c-e，2-3

第16窟　第二十二幅，b-e，6-9

第16窟

（立佛洞）

公元460-470年

第二十三幅

第 16 窟　明窗东壁佛龛坐佛　Seated Buddha, East Wall Niche of Upper Window

第 16 窟　第二十四幅，明窗东壁二佛并坐像　Two Seated Buddhas Side by Side, East Wall of Upper Window

第16窟
（立佛洞）
公元460-470年

第二十五幅

第 16 窟　明窗二佛并坐龛右侧化生童子与拱尾反首狮　Kumara Upa-paduka and Lion with Back-Turning Head and Arching Tail, Right Side of Two Seated Buddhas Niche of Upper Window

第 16-1 窟　第二十六幅，东壁二佛并坐龛　Niche with Two Seated Buddhas, East Wall

第一幅

a	b	c	d	e	f

440 – 441

第二幅

442 – 445

第三幅

446 – 447

第四幅

448 – 449

第五幅

450

第六幅

451

第七幅

452 – 455

第八幅

456 – 457

第九幅

458 – 459

第十幅

460 – 461

第十一幅

462 – 463

第十二幅

464

第十三幅

465

第十四幅

466 – 467

第十五幅

468 – 469

第十六幅

470 – 473

474 – 475

第十七幅

476 – 477

第十八幅

478 – 479

第十九幅

480 – 481

第二十幅

482 – 483

第二十一幅

484 – 485

第二十二幅

486

第二十三幅

487

第二十四幅

第二十五幅

488 – 491

第 17 窟
（弥勒三尊洞）
公元 460-470 年

第一幅

第 17 窟　主菩萨头部　Head of Central Bodhisattva

第 17 窟
（弥勒三尊洞）
公元 460-470 年

第
二
幅

第 17 窟　西壁立佛　Standing Buddha, West Wall

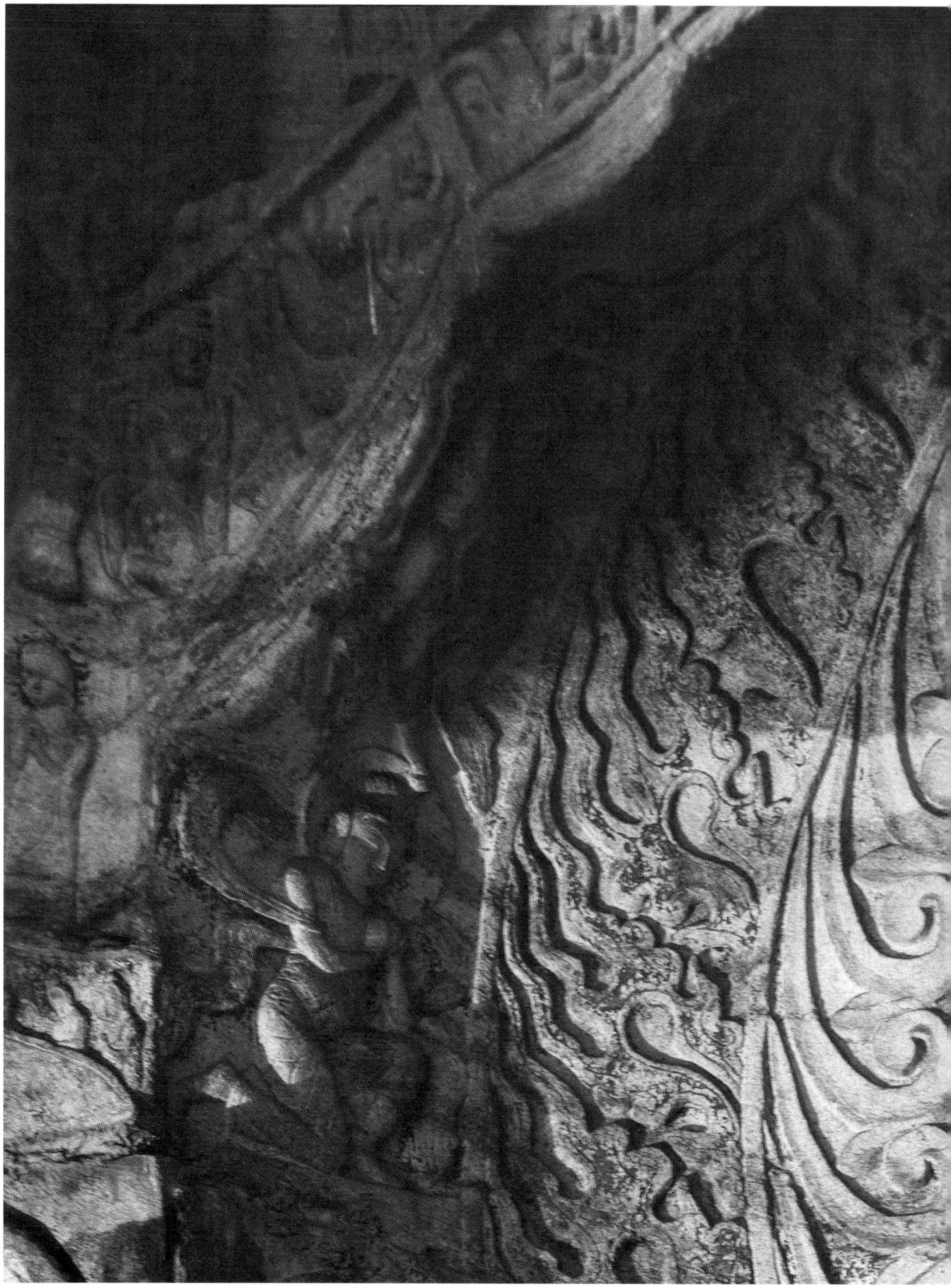

第 17 窟　第二幅，a-e，1-2

第 17 窟　第三幅，西壁立佛头部特写　Head of Standing Buddha, West Wall

第 17 窟
（弥勒三尊洞）
公元 460-470 年

第四幅

第 17 窟　西壁立佛背光右半　Right Side of Standing Buddha's Aureola, West Wall

第 17 窟　第五幅，西壁佛龛内右侧供养天　Right Side Offering Deva, West Wall Niche

第 17 窟　第六幅，西壁佛龛内左侧供养天　Left Side Offering Deva, West Wall Niche

第 17 窟
（弥勒三尊洞）
公元 460-470 年

第
七
幅

第 17 窟　东壁坐佛　Seated Buddha, East Wall

第17窟 第七幅，a-c，1-2

第 17 窟　第八幅，东壁佛像头像特写　Head of Seated Buddha, East Wall

第 17 窟
（弥勒三尊洞）
公元 460-470 年

第
九
幅

第 17 窟　东壁盝形龛龛楣格内　Tympanum of Truncated-Tent Shaped Niche, East Wall

第17窟
(弥勒三尊洞)
公元460-470年

第
十
幅

第 17 窟　东壁盝形龛龛楣格内　Tympanum of Truncated-Tent Shaped Niche, East Wall

第 17 窟
（弥勒三尊洞）
公元 460-470 年

第十一幅

第 17 窟　东壁盝形龛龛楣格内　Tympanum of Truncated-Tent Shaped Niche, East Wall

第 17 窟　第十二幅，东壁佛龛内右侧供养天　Right Side Offering Deva, East Wall Niche

第 17 窟　第十三幅，东壁佛龛内左侧供养天　Left Side Offering Deva, East Wall Niche

第 17 窟　第十四幅，东壁上层　Upper Portion, East Wall

第 17 窟
（弥勒三尊洞）
公元 460-470 年

第十五幅

第 17 窟　东壁北侧二佛并坐龛　Niche with Two Seated Buddhas, North Side of East Wall

第 17 窟
（弥勒三尊洞）
公元 460-470 年

第十六幅

第 17 窟　南壁窟门东侧佛龛　Niche East of Entrance Gateway, South Wall

第 17 窟　第十六幅，b-d，2-3

第 17 窟　第十六幅，f，2

第17窟
（弥勒三尊洞）
公元460-470年

第十七幅

第 17 窟　南壁窟门东侧右胁侍菩萨　Right Side Attendant Bodhisattva, East of Entrance Gateway of South Wall

第17窟
（弥勒三尊洞）
公元460-470年

第十八幅

第 17 窟　南壁窟门东侧佛龛左胁侍菩萨　Left Side Attendant Bodhisattva, East of Entrance Gateway of South Wall

第 17 窟　第十九幅，南壁佛龛龛楣内禅定坐佛　Seated Buddha in Meditation, Tympanum of South Wall Niche

第 17 窟　第二十幅，明窗东壁二佛并坐龛　Niche with Two Seated Buddhas, East Wall of Upper Window

第 17 窟　第二十一幅，明窗东壁交脚菩萨像　Cross-Ankled Bodhisattva, East Wall of Upper Window

第 17 窟
（弥勒三尊洞）
公元 460-470 年

第二十二幅

第 17 窟　明窗东壁交脚菩萨像　Cross-Ankled Bodhisattva, East Wall of Upper Window

第 17 窟　第二十三幅，明窗东壁龛外右上隅供养天　Offering Devas, Upper Right Corner Outside East Wall Niche of Upper Window

第 17 窟　第二十四幅，明窗东壁中部北侧思惟菩萨　Pensive Bodhisattva, Central North Portion of East Wall of Upper Window

第 17 窟
（弥勒三尊洞）
公元 460-470 年

第二十五幅

第 17 窟　明窗西壁龛像　Niche with Statues, West Wall of Upper Window

第 17 窟　第二十五幅，a-c，2-3

第一幅

496 – 501

502 – 503

第二幅

504 – 505

第三幅

第四幅

506 – 509

510 – 511

第五幅

第六幅

512 – 515

516 – 517

第七幅

518 – 519

第八幅

520 – 521

第九幅

522

第十幅

523

第十一幅

524

第十二幅

525

第十三幅

第十四幅

526 – 531

532 – 533

第十五幅

第 18 窟
（立三佛洞）
公元 460-470 年

第
一
幅

第 18 窟　内景　Interior

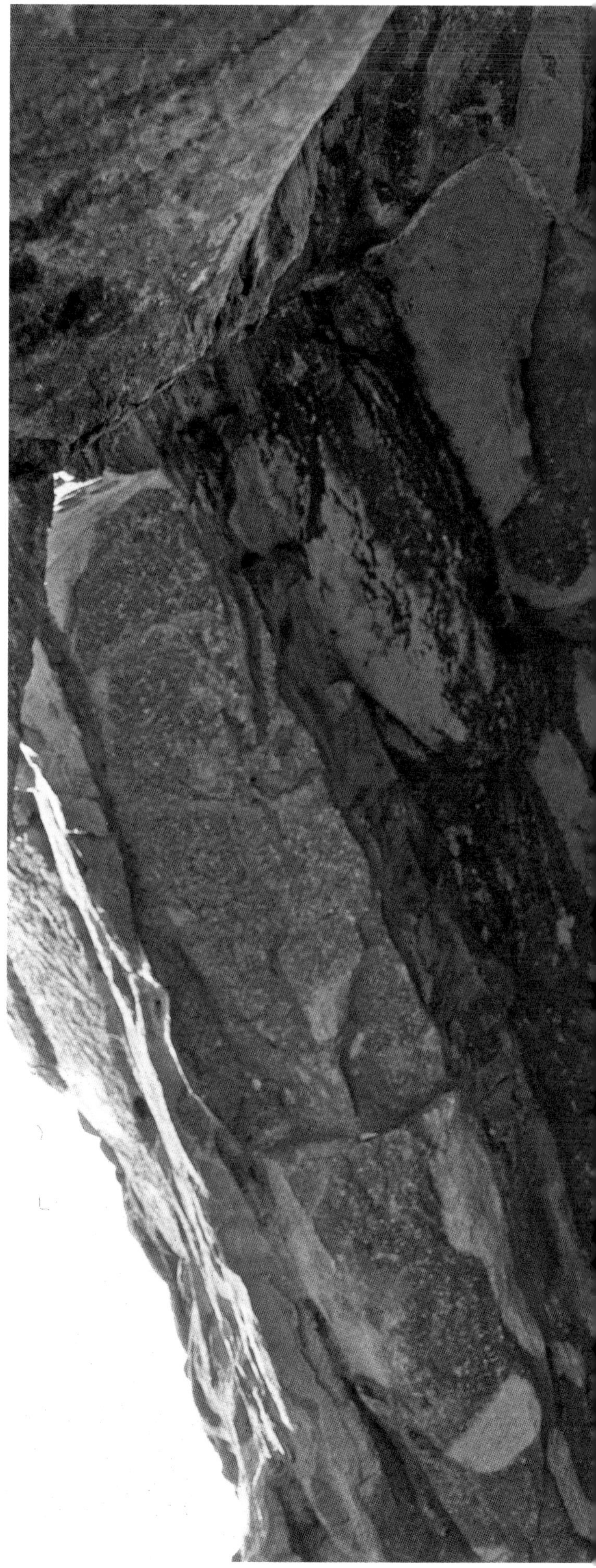

第18窟　第一幅，c-f，1-3

第18窟　第一幅，a-e，6-8

第 18 窟
（立三佛洞）
公元 460-470 年

第二幅

第 18 窟　北壁主像头部特写　Head of Central Buddha, North Wall

第 18 窟　第三幅，北壁主佛左手与东壁弟子像　Left Hand of North Wall Central Buddha and East Wall Disciples

第 18 窟
（立三佛洞）
公元 460-470 年

第
四
幅

第 18 窟　北壁佛像袈裟　Detail of Central Buddha's Kasaya, North Wall

第18窟　第四幅，a-d，2-4

第18窟
（立三佛洞）
公元460-470年

第
五
幅

第 18 窟　北壁佛手侧面儒童本生故事图　Scene of Dipankara Jataka, Next to Central Buddha's Hand, North Wall

第18窟
（立三佛洞）
公元460-470年

第
六
幅

第 18 窟　东壁胁侍佛　Standing Buddha, East Wall

第18窟　第六幅，b，2

第 18 窟　第六幅，c，3

第18窟
（立三佛洞）
公元460-470年

第
七
幅

第 18 窟　东壁　East Wall

第18窟
（立三佛洞）
公元460-470年

第
八
幅

第 18 窟　东壁胁侍菩萨头像　Head of Attendant Bodhisattva, East Wall

第18窟
（立三佛洞）
公元460-470年

第
九
幅

第 18 窟　东壁胁侍菩萨头像　Head of Attendant Bodhisattva, East Wall

第 18 窟　第十幅，北壁弟子头像　Head of Disciple, North Wall

第 18 窟　第十三幅，东壁弟子像　Disciple, East Wall

第 18 窟
（立三佛洞）
公元 460-470 年

第十四幅

第 18 窟　南壁西側龕像　West Niche, South Wall

第 18 窟　第十四幅，h-l，4-7

第18窟　第十四幅，h-i，4

第 18 窟　第十四幅，h-i，6-7

第18窟

（立三佛洞）

公元460-470年

第十五幅

第 18 窟　南壁东龛右胁侍菩萨　Right Side Attendant Bodhisattva, East Niche of South Wall

a b c

1
2
3
4
5

第一幅

538 – 541

第二幅

542 – 543

第三幅

544 – 545

第四幅

546 – 547

第五幅

548 – 549

第六幅

550 – 551

第七幅

552 – 553

第八幅

554 – 555

第九幅

556 – 557

第十幅

558 – 561

第十一幅

562 – 563

第十二幅

564 – 565

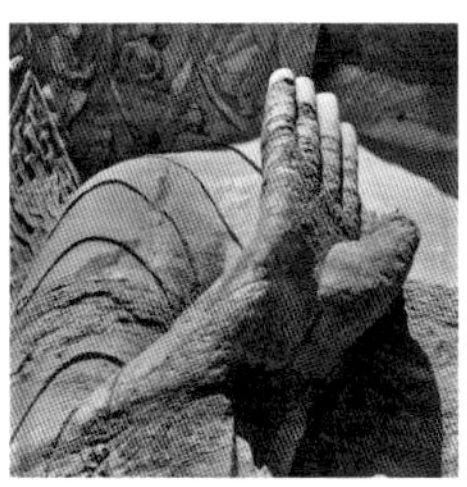

第十三幅

566 – 567

第十四幅

568 – 569

570 – 571

第十五幅

第十六幅

572 – 575

第 19 窟

（宝生佛洞）

公元 460-470 年

第一幅

第 19 窟 内景　Interior

第19窟　第一幅，b-c，2-3

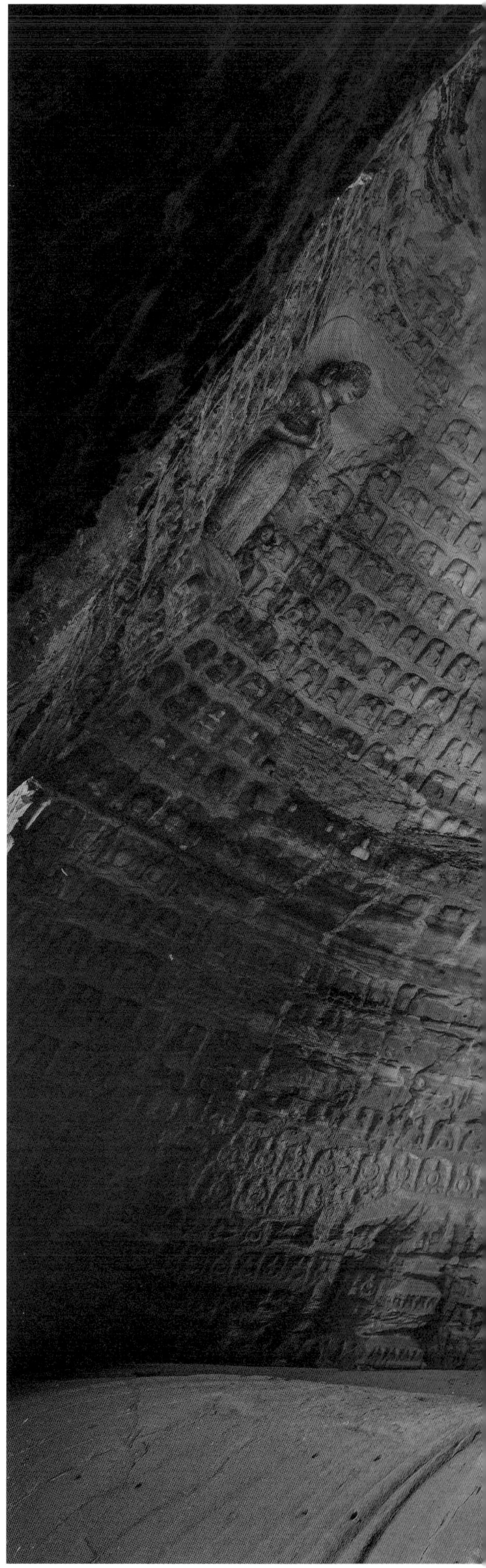

第 19 窟　第二幅，北壁主佛　Central Buddha, North Wall

第19窟
（宝生佛洞）
公元460-470年

第
三
幅

第 19 窟 北壁主像头部　Head of Central Buddha, North Wall

第19窟
（宝生佛洞）
公元460-470年

第四幅

第 19 窟 内景　Interior

第 19 窟　第五幅，南壁罗睺罗因缘故事图　Scene of "Vyakarana of Rahula", South Wall

第 19 窟

（宝生佛洞）

公元 460-470 年

第六幅

第 19 窟 南壁凿洞 Chiseled Opening, South Wall

第19窟
（宝生佛洞）
公元460-470年

第
七
幅

第 19 窟 南壁窟门东侧小沙弥 Samanera, East Side of Entrance Gateway of South Wall

第19窟
（宝生佛洞）
公元460-470年

第
八
幅

第 19-1 窟 右胁侍菩萨 Right Side Attendant Bodhisattva

第 19 窟
（宝生佛洞）
公元 460-470 年

第九幅

第 19-1 窟 右胁侍菩萨头像 Head of Right Side Attendant Bodhisattva

第19窟
（宝生佛洞）
公元460-470年

第十幅

第 19-2 窟 倚坐佛 Throne-Seated Buddha

第 19-2 窟　第十幅，a-c，4-5

第 19-2 窟　第十一幅，佛头特写　Head of Buddha

第 19 窟
（宝生佛洞）
公元 460-470 年

第
十
二
幅

第 19-2 窟 佛手　Hand of Buddha

第 19-2 窟　第十三幅，佛像右侧背光右侧供养天　Offering Deva, Right Side of Buddha's Aureola

第19窟
(宝生佛洞)
公元460-470年

第
十
四
幅

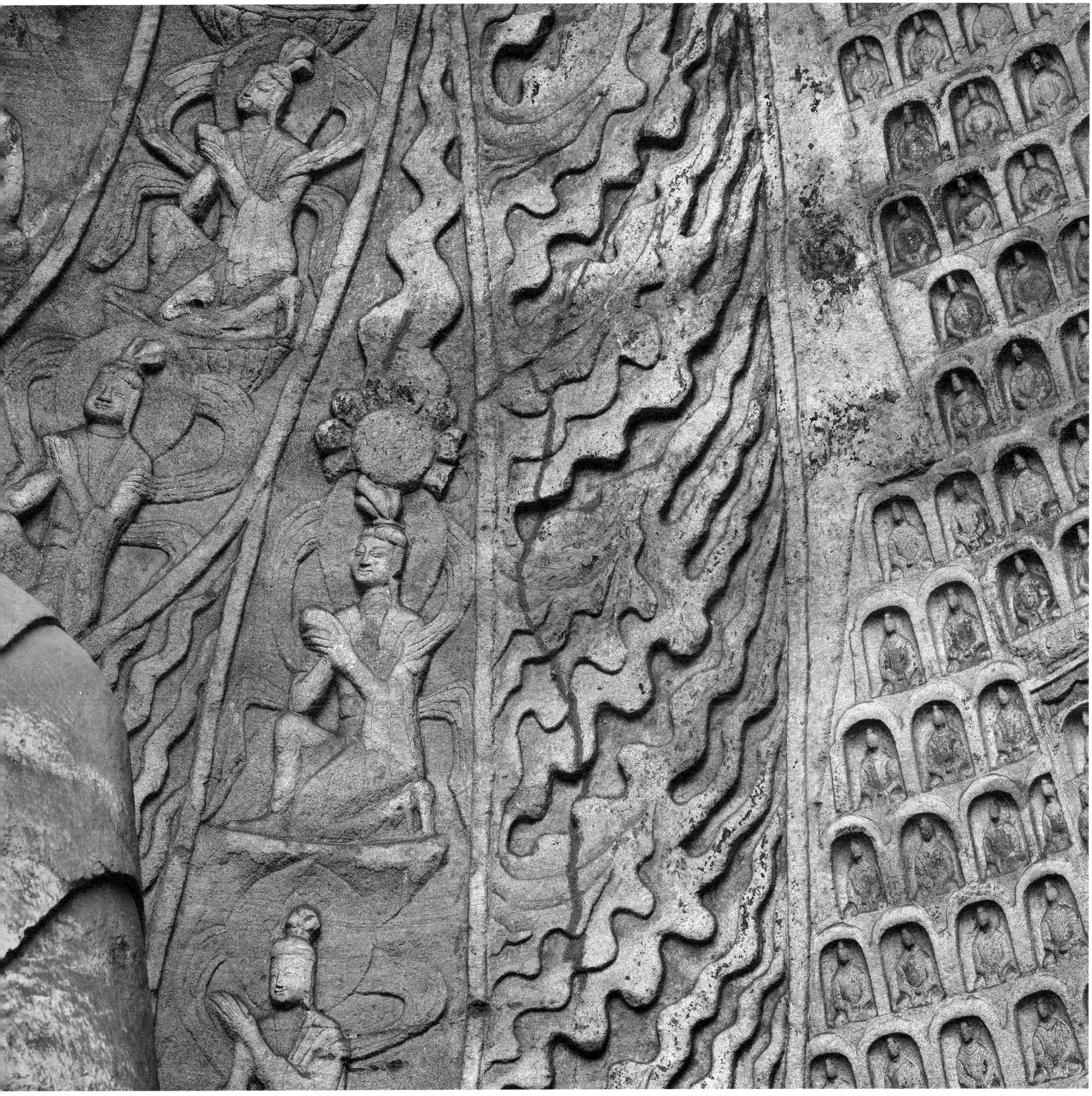

第 19-2 窟 佛像背光左侧供养天　Offering Deva, Left Side of Buddha's Aureola

第19窟
（宝生佛洞）
公元460-470年

第
十
五
幅

第 19-2 窟 左胁侍菩萨 Left Side Attendant Bodhisattva

第19窟
（宝生佛洞）
公元460-470年

第十六幅

第 19-2 窟 窟门左壁龛像 Niches with Statues, Left Wall of Entrance Gateway

第19-2窟　第十六幅，b-c，2

578 – 579

第一幅

580 – 581

第二幅

第三幅

582 – 585

586 – 587

第四幅

588

第五幅

589

第六幅

第20窟
（白佛爷洞）
公元460-470年

第
一
幅

第 20 窟　全景　Full Front View

第 20 窟　第二幅，主佛上半身　Upper Body of Central Buddha

第20窟
（白佛爷洞）
公元460-470年

第
三
幅

第 20 窟　主佛侧面　Left Side of Central Buddha

第 20 窟　第三幅，c，2-3

第20窟
（白佛爷洞）
公元460-470年

第
四
幅

第 20 窟　东立佛　East Side Standing Buddha

第 20 窟　第五幅，主尊佛像背光右侧　Right Side of Central Buddha's Aureola

第 20 窟　第六幅，主尊佛像背光左侧　Left Side of Central Buddha's Aureola

第一幅

594 – 597

第二幅

598 – 599

第三幅

600 – 601

第四幅

602

第五幅

603

第六幅

604 – 605

第七幅

606 – 609

610 – 611

第八幅

第九幅

612 – 613

614 – 615

第十幅

第十一幅

616 – 617

618 – 619

第十二幅

620 – 621

第十三幅

第十四幅

622 – 625

第十五幅

626 – 627

第十六幅

628 – 629

第十七幅

630 – 631

第十八幅

632 – 633

第十九幅

634 – 635

第21-37窟
（西部诸窟）
公元494-525年

第
一
幅

第 21 窟　东壁盝形龛　Truncated-Tent Shaped Niche, East Wall

第21窟　第一幅，b-c，4

第21窟　第一幅，d-e，2

第 21-37 窟
（西部诸窟）
公元 494-525 年

第
二
幅

第 21 窟　东壁交脚菩萨头部　Head of Cross-Ankled Bodhisattva, East Wall

第 21-37 窟
（西部诸窟）
公元 494-525 年

第三幅

第 23 窟　窟顶飞天　Apsaras, Cave Ceiling

第 25 窟　第四幅，窟顶飞天　Apsara, Cave Ceiling

第 25 窟　第五幅，窟顶飞天　Apsara, Cave Ceiling

第 21-37 窟
（西部诸窟）
公元 494-525 年

第
六
幅

第 25-2 窟 西壁弟子与菩萨 Bodhisattva and Disciple, West Wall

第 21-37 窟
（西部诸窟）
公元 494-525 年

第
七
幅

第 26 窟　东壁　East Wall

第 26 窟　第七幅，b-d，4-5

第21-37窟
（西部诸窟）
公元494-525年

第八幅

第 26 窟 窟顶平棊 Coffered Ceiling

第 21-37 窟
（西部诸窟）
公元 494-525 年

第九幅

第27窟　西壁　West Wall

第 21-37 窟
（西部诸窟）
公元 494-525 年

第
十
幅

第 27 窟　西壁佛龛拱尾　Ends of Tympanum, West Wall Niches

第 21-37 窟
（西部诸窟）
公元 494-525 年

第十一幅

第 29 窟　东壁　East Wall

第 29 窟　第十二幅，窟顶平棊　Coffered Ceiling

第 21-37 窟
（西部诸窟）
公元 494-525 年

第
十
三
幅

21 第 29 窟　西壁下层佛龛拱尾　Ends of Tympanum, Lower Portion of West Wall

第 21-37 窟
（西部诸窟）
公元 494-525 年

第十四幅

第 34 窟　西壁佛龛左上隅飞天　Apsara, Upper Left Corner, West Wall Niche

第 34 窟　第十四幅，b-c，1-3

第 35 窟　西壁盝形龛楣外右上隅　Upper Right Corner Outside Truncated-Tent Shaped Niche, West Wall

第 35 窟 第十六幅，西壁逾城出家故事图 Scene of "Great Departure", West Wall

第21-37窟
（西部诸窟）
公元494-525年

第
十
七
幅

第 35 窟　东壁佛涅槃故事图　Scene of Parinirvana, East Wall

第 35 窟　第十八幅，南壁降魔成道故事图局部　Detail of "Assault on Buddha by Mara" Scene, South Wall

第21-37窟
（西部诸窟）
公元494-525年

第十九幅

第 37 窟　西壁乘象投胎故事图　Scene of "Mayadevi's White Elephant Dream", West Wall

2012–2022

赵富义、宫品仁

国人首次用大画幅黑白胶片摄影技术对云冈石窟进行系统性拍摄。本书收录二人的摄影作品 200 余幅。

Chinese photographers Zhao Fuyi and Gong Pinren are the firsts in systematically documenting Yungang with large format black and white film photography. More than 200 photos of their works are included in this publication.

2013–2019

张焯主编《云冈石窟全集》出版工程历时近 7 年，凡 20 卷，用图 12710 张，收录造像 59265 身，编号洞窟 45 个，保存了一份迄今最完整、最权威的云冈石窟影像谱系资料

The seven-year publishing project of *A Complete Collection of the Yungang Grottoes*, edited by Zhang Zhuo, comprised of 20 volumes, included 12,710 photos illustrating 59,265 Buddhist images and documenting 45 caves, thus constituted the most complete and authoritative resources to the date of the Yungang Grottoes in visual images.

21 世纪前 10 年

云冈石窟摄影美术著作蓬勃发展，以中国石窟雕塑全集编辑委员会编《中国美术分类全集 · 中国石窟雕塑全集 · 云冈》（第三卷：李治国主编）（2001）、冯骥才主编《中国大同雕塑全集 · 云冈石窟雕刻卷》（2010）等摄影图集为代表

Publications of photographic works of the Yungang Grottoes were thriving, represented by catalogues such as *A Complete Collection of Sculptural Art in Chinese Grottoes: Yungang*, edited by Li Zhiguo in 2001; and *A Complete Collection of Sculptural Art in Datong: the Yungang Grottoes Volume* by Feng Jicai in 2010.

2000

20 世纪 50 年代以来

开始出现由山西文物保护研究机构编著的一系列著作和图录

A series of publications and catalogues were published by cultural heritage conservation and research institutions in Shanxi Province.

1950

1938—1944 水野清一、长广敏雄

七年间，日本京都大学人文科学研究所的水野清一、长广敏雄对云冈石窟进行深入调查，并将其摄影、实测、线描、拓片、论文等研究成果结集为 16 卷本《云冈石窟——公元五世纪中国北部佛教石窟寺院的考古学调查报告》

Japanese scholars Mizuno Seiichi and Nagahiro Toshio led the Mission of the Tohobunka Kenkyusho (Institute of Oriental Culture) of Kyoto University to Yungang Grottoes and conducted seven investigations. All their findings and results, including photographs, drawings, survey plans, rubbings and essays were compiled into a monumental sixteen-volume, thirty-two-book publication: *Yun-Kang: the Buddhist Cave-mples of the Fifth Century A.D. in North China.*

1937 （美）吉尔伯特 · 格罗斯文纳

拍摄了大量的云冈石窟照片，并于 1938 年 3 月在美国《国家地理》杂志上出版

A series of photographs of the Yungang Grottoes taken by Gilbert Grosvenor, Editor of National Geographic Magazine, were published in Volume 73, Number 3 Issue of the magazine in March 1938.

1933 梁思成、林徽因、刘敦桢等

中国营造学社同人考察云冈石窟，对石窟展开调查与摄影

Chinese architect Liang Sicheng and his colleagues at the Society for Research in Chinese Architecture, including Lin Huiyin and Liu Dunzhen, visited the Yungang Grottoes and did in field research and photography.

1926 （日）长盘大定、关野贞

二人合著《支那佛教史迹》，全书收录云冈石窟照片 119 幅

Japanese art historians Tokiwa Daijo and Sekino Tadashi collaborated in publishing *Shina bunka shiseki (Chinese Cultural Heritage)* which included 119 photos of the Yungang Grottoes.

1925 （瑞典）喜龙仁

出版《中国雕刻——从五世纪到十四世纪》（四卷本），书中收录云冈石窟照片 66 幅

Swedish art historian Osvald Sirén included 66 photos of the Yungang Grottoes in his four-volume *Chinese Sculpture from the Fifth to the Fourteenth Century.*

1925 （日）外村氏

将拍摄的云冈石窟照片集结成册，出版《大同石佛大观》

A Japanese photographer named Mr. Sotomura compiled his photos of the Yungang Grottoes into a book titled *Daido sekibutsu tenbo (The Great View of Datong Stone Buddhas).*

1910 （日）山本明

拍摄了大量的中国名胜古迹影像，并将有关云冈石窟的照片收录于《云冈石窟》（1921）和《震旦旧迹图汇·第一编·云冈石窟》（1924）

Japanese photographer Yamamoto Akira took a series of photographs of ancient Chinese heritage sites, and published photographs of the Yungang Grottoes in *Unko sekkutsu (Rock-carvings from the Yun-kang Caves)* in 1921, and *Shintan kyuuseki zui Unko sekkutsu (A Pictorial Collection of Chinese Ancient Sites Volume 1: the Yun-Kang Caves)* in 1924.

1907 （法）沙畹

拍摄了大量的云冈石窟照片，择取其中 78 幅收录于《华北考古记》

Edouard Chavannes, the French sinologist, took numerous photos of the Yungang Grottoes and published 78 of them in *Mission archeologique dans la Chine septentrionale.*

1902 （日）伊东忠太

拍摄下了云冈石窟最早的照片

Ito Chuta, a Japanese architect, took the first photographs of the Yungang Grottoes.

1900

图书在版编目（CIP）数据

云冈大画幅 / 云冈研究院，三晋出版社编；赵富义，宫品仁摄影．— 太原：三
晋出版社，2023.10
ISBN 978-7-5457-2743-2

Ⅰ．①云… Ⅱ．①云… ②三… ③赵… ④宫… Ⅲ．①云冈石窟—画册 Ⅳ．
① K879.222

中国国家版本馆 CIP 数据核字（2023）第 169377 号

云冈大画幅 | 问佛 NO.2

编　　者　云冈研究院　三晋出版社
主　　编　张　焯
副 主 编　赵昆雨　赵富义
摄　　影　赵富义　宫品仁
撰　　文　张　焯　赵昆雨　介子平
翻　　译　吴　洁　叶　南

出版统筹　莫晓东
责任编辑　张　婷
助理编辑　王　宇　周瑞程
书籍设计　张　宇
责任印制　李佳音

出 版 者　山西出版传媒集团·三晋出版社
地　　址　太原市建设南路 21 号
电　　话　0351 - 4956036（总编室）
　　　　　0351 - 4922203（印制部）
网　　址　http://www.sjcbs.cn

经 销 者　新华书店
承 印 者　北京雅昌艺术印刷有限公司

开　　本　889mm×1194mm　1/12
印　　张　53
字　　数　650 千字
版　　次　2023 年 10 月　第 1 版
印　　次　2023 年 10 月　第 1 次印刷
书　　号　ISBN 978-7-5457-2743-2
定　　价　1280.00 元（全二册）